SEAN DORMAN, as a boy of
Irish public school, was awarded
and the English master regularly
Form. He became editor of the
winner of an essay competition
Great Britain and Ireland. After gr

as a freelance journalist in London, naving articles published in
some twenty British and Irish periodicals. He also ghosted half
a dozen non-fiction books for a publisher. He had a burlesque
of Chekhov staged by the Dublin Gate Theatre, a radio play
broadcast by Radio Eireann, and he published a few short stories,
one being broadcast by the BBC. For five and a half years
in Dublin he published a literary, theatre and art magazine,
Commentary. In England, from 1957 until a few years ago, he
ran the Sean Dorman Manuscript Society for mutual criticism, a
Society still run by others under the same name and listed in *The
Writers' and Artists' Year Book*. His magazine *Writing*, also
listed during its career in 'The Year Book', was founded in 1959,
and sold after twenty-six years. While his family was growing
up, he had to seek a more regular income, and taught secondary
school French and junior German for some twenty-five years. To
make up for lost time, between 1983 and 1993 he wrote and
published, under the imprint of his Raffeen Press, eleven books.
They embraced novels, autobiography, essays, a three-act play,
theatre criticism, short-stories and a solitary poem. Many of the
books were re-writes or extensions, now allowed to go out of
print, so the present tally is six. Five of these have been included
in his three-volume hardback, *The Selected Works of Sean
Dorman*, now gradually finding its way into national and
university libraries throughout the world.

COVER GIRL
*For my beautiful Irish compatriot,
FIONA -- with myself! The author.*

Also by Sean Dorman

BRIGID AND THE MOUNTAIN
a novel

RED ROSES FOR JENNY
a novel

THE MADONNA
a novel

THE STRONG MAN
a play

PHYSICIANS, PRIESTS & PHYSICISTS
essays

and published by The Raffeen Press

Further copies of
PORTRAIT OF MY YOUTH
may be obtained through
Waterstone's and other good bookshops.
Also from The Raffeen Press
Union Place, Fowey, Cornwall PL23 1BY.

PORTRAIT OF MY YOUTH

Sean Dorman

THE RAFFEEN PRESS

Cover montage: JOHN ALLMARK
Photograph: Jim Matthews
Street scene and graphics: John Allmark

PORTRAIT OF MY YOUTH
A RAFFEEN PRESS BOOK 0 9518119 9 1

PRINTING HISTORY
In paperback (black and white illustrations) 1992
Reissued (in three-volume hardback
The Selected Works of Sean Dorman,
colour and black and white illustrations) 1993
Reissued in paperback 1995

Printed and bound in Great Britain by Short Run Press Ltd, Exeter.

PORTRAIT OF MY YOUTH

Chapter One
British Raj

I was born at number nineteen Dykes Parade, then a nursing-home, in the City of Cork, half way along the south coast of Ireland. When? Ah . . . Let it suffice that I *was* born, that is, I neither sprang from the head of Zeus nor rose from the sea. I was given the name of 'John' (or Jack) after my paternal godfather, Surgeon General John Cotter Dorman, CMG, of the Medical Corps of the British Army, on his retirement living at Rampart House in the ancient town of Kinsale, near Cork. (His son, Brigidier Edward Dorman, DSO, commanded the 4th/7th Royal Irish Dragoon Guards, as well as a cavalry brigade; and his younger daughter married a Devonian, General Sir Walter Venning, Quarter-master General of the British Forces.) However, there was no soldiering in *me*, so my maternal and nationalist godfather, Dr Lennox Robinson, playwright and director, with Lady Gregory, W B Yeats and others, of the Irish National Theatre, the Abbey Theatre, ultimately gained the day when he insisted in changing 'John' to its Irish equivalent, 'Sean'. In her diary, my paternal grandmother, living at the other main Dorman home in Kinsale, 'Raffeen', seeing me for the first time as a newly-born, records, 'A very fine large child, and slept nearly all day.' Rather slack of me, I feel. I should have been sitting up, writing.

Though the above may appear to indicate that we were, from the beginning, an Anglo-Irish family, in fact we originated in France. Jean de Dormans, Bishop and Count de Beauvais, Cardinal, and Deputy Chancellor of France, was the founder of the College of Beauvais. When he died on 7 November, 1374, he was buried before the High Altar there. Earlier than he was Guillaume de Dormans, Chancellor of France in 1371. When he died on 11 July, 1373, he was buried in the Choir of the Church of the Carthusians. Another Guillaume de Dormans was Bishop of Meaux and Archbishop of Sans, or Sais. When he died in October 1405, he was buried in the Chapel of the College of Beauvais. So also was Jeanne de Dormans in 1407. She was married twice, first to Pierre de Rochfort, Knight; and, second, to Phillibert, Lord of Paillart and of Tilly. At Versailles there are various de Dormans fourteenth century tombs, numbers 298, 299 (these are copies; the originals are in the College de Dormans de Beauvais), and 1,262. In Paris, Jean de Dormans, Lord of Nozay, St Reiny and Herporte, Ambassador from King Louis XI to the Pope, on his death on 11 November 1472 was buried in the Choir of the Carthusians. Guillaume de Dormans, Lord of Nozay, etc, when he died on 5 January, 1507, was buried in the vaults of the Holy Innocents in Paris. Colombe de Bonnay, wife of Bernard de Dormans, Lord of Nozay, was buried in the cemetery of the Holy Innocents. Her will is dated 1478. But the nearest in date to the Dormans appearing in County Cork, having foolishly become Protestants and having to flee from France together with over half a million other Huguenots, was Suzanne de Dormans. She married Francois de St Bausseu, Lord of Berlize and Steward of the King. When she died on 5 August, 1638, she was buried in the Church of the Franciscans, Paris, with her father, mother, and three sisters.

The first recorded Dorman (we dropped the 'de' and the 's') in County Cork was Richard Dorman of Monygormy, who was born around 1670, no long time after Suzanne, allowing for the hurly-burly of flight and its upset to records. My cousin in Looe, Cornwall, Stephen Dorman, who has looked through the two wills (1745 and 1749) of Richard Dorman, tells me that he owned a quantity of land and, together with someone else, raised sufficient money to rebuild Carrigaline Church in County Cork. He possessed a haggard (barn?) of corn, and had substantial numbers of horses, sheep and cows. Shade of Jean de Dormans, Count de Beauvais, Cardinal! Let this serve as a warning to any Catholic toying with the idea of becoming a Protestant. It *can* lead from Cardinal to cows.

My parents transferred me to India when I was about six weeks old. Thus I became one of a relatively small coterie of Europeans ruling over a sub-continent of hundreds of millions of brown people. I found nothing astonishing in this astonishing state of affairs; I had never known any other.

Since I have no exact idea in what order events occurred, I divide them into 'The Plains' and 'The Hills'. My life in India oscillated between these two points. It was the plains in The Cold Weather, that is, when the afternoon temperature rose to that of a good British or Irish summer day, seventy degrees Fahrenheit or twenty-one degrees Celsius (though capable of falling below freezing point at night). It was the hills in The Hot Weather, when the temperature down in the plains was able to rise to over a hundred and twenty degrees Fahrenheit (forty-nine Celsius) in the shade. Then the sun became an unendurable furnace belting down its fires upon the broad mostly dried up beds of the five rivers of the Punjab, until the monsoon came to fill them. In the cold weather it was mostly Lahore or Ambala; in the hot weather, Simla or Dalhousie.

On arrival in the plains, my parents stayed initially with a friend who, like my father, was an engineer in the Roads and Buildings side of the Public Works Department. This latter was known by the initials 'P. W. D.' The P. W. D. was second only to the Civil Service. It was whispered in the P. W. D. that the Civil Service, which had in its power to recommend the bestowal of knighthoods, itself practically hogged the lot.

My mother, coming into breakfast the first day and observing the cloudless Punjab sky, remarked, 'What a lovely morning!' Her host politely agreed. On the second day she said, 'What a lovely morning!' Again agreed. On the third day he burst out laughing. 'You'll soon stop saying that. It's always a lovely morning — unless we're in the monsoons.'

The first house I remember was 'Raffeen' in Lahore. 'Raffeen' was named after the family home at Kinsale in County Cork. I, and my sister Eileen when she was born (in Simla), were first looked after by a succession of ayahs, Indian nurses wearing saris. One such ayah, in order to keep Eileen as a baby quiet, was discovered to be giving her opium. My mother flew at the ayah's throat, and the ayah fled. After that my mother would have no more of ayahs and engaged a Eurasian nurse, known to us an Nanny.

Nanny, of mixed European and Asian stock, was brown, was a Christian, wore European clothes, and spoke and wrote in English.

9

I never heard the term 'Anglo-Indian' in any context until I came 'Home', as Great Britain always was called. As far as I was concerned there were only three sorts of people in the universe, Europeans, Indians, and Eurasians like Nanny. Eurasians were superior to Indians, but were a sort of inferior European. Nanny loved us dearly and never let a day pass without informing us that we were the worst behaved children she had ever had to look after, comparing us in detail and to our enormous disadvantage with all those other children she had had to look after. It soon became apparent to us that we were the unworthy last in a line of otherwise Super Children, with whom it was useless even to attempt to compete.

I associate Nanny with her Bible, her prayer-book and her hymn-book, all bound in black and stacked in that order on her bedside table. She made clear to us that dreadful consequences would flow upon anyone who placed a book on top of a Bible, unless that book were a prayer-book, a hymn-book or another Bible. There were occasional visits from one or other of her two sisters, Agnes and Lizzie, both also missionary-educated. Lizzie was thin with a deeply pock-marked face, I suppose from smallpox.

One day in Lahore Nanny took Eileen and me into a room where our mother was lying in bed. Nanny pushed and cajoled us into kissing a menacing object that she held in her arms wrapped in a blanket. I pulled back my mouth hurriedly as I got the impression that the object's face was covered with powder. Presumably I smelt the baby-powder and imagined the rest. The object was my newly-born younger sister, Maureen. This would mean that I was about four years of age at the time, and that Eileen was about two.

When we had curry, which seemed to me hot enough, Nanny would extract fiery-looking chillis, some red some green, from a bottle to add to the combustion on her plate. If soft-boiled eggs were on the menu, she would cut her bread and butter into thin fingers. With fascinated disgust I watched her eat her egg by dipping the fingers into it and thence transferring the yellow-dripping morsels into her mouth. We were never allowed to spread our butter thickly; butter was expensive, according to Nanny. I still can feel the horror with which I watched a boy guest pile the butter on the halves of his scones. I did not dare to look at Nanny, but tremblingly awaited an explosion that never came.

As tiny children we were always 'pottied' in the bathroom. On completing our 'business', as Nanny called it, we circulated round gravely examining and discussing one another's achievements. The bath took the form of a sunken rectangle in the brick floor, filled for the occasion by the bishti wallah. I spell all such Indian words as I pronounced them; as far as speaking was concerned, we were bi-lingual in English and Hindustani, but wrote only in English. The bishti wallah brought in the water on his back in a bag made of hide. He decanted its contents sidways and downwards into the bath, controlling the flow by squeezing on the nozzle.

The only piece of furniture was the commode. This was emptied from time to time by the mayther. The mayther was an Untouchable, the lowest of the low, barely a human being, and could do the most degrading things like emptying commodes and eating European food. I often saw him holding out his tin plate at the kitchen back door. The kitmergars (waiters) first scraped the remains of our meat course on to the plate, and then straight on top of it the sweet course. In addition, when we were allowed as an occasional treat to evening-dine with our parents, we started with soup and ended with biscuits, cheese and fruit. Our sticky fingers we washed in finger-bowls, and dried them with the little muslin doilies, weighted down with beads, that had covered each finger-bowl. The excellent cooking was all done on nothing more than two charcoal braziers standing on the kitchen floor, at which the two cooks/waiters squatted.

I said that we were bi-lingual in English and Hindustani. That is what we as children called it — Hindustani. Oh, I had heard the words 'Urdu' and 'Punjabi' mentioned by my parents, but was quite vague as to how it all fitted together. Only fairly recently, on meeting an Indian girl in London, did I make the effort to clear up the position. I spoke to her such smattering of Hindustani as remained to me, and she informed me that I was speaking Urdu. I then asked what other main languages were spoken in the Punjab, and she replied that Hindi and Punjabi were spoken. I then asked why it was that I never had any feeling that I couldn't communicate with anyone, of course within the compass of understanding of a small child. She replied that she herself spoke only Urdu, but could understand Hindi or Punjabi if they were spoken to her. My elderly 'Concise Oxford Dictionary' tells me that, among other things, Hindustani is just another name for Urdu; and that Urdu is Hindi mixed with Arabic, Persian, etc. — in short, the language manufactured by the pre-British-Raj Moslem conquerors.

It was in The Plains that I had my first reading lesson at the, by modern standards, late age of six. My father took me on his knee. He held up before me the illustrated reading-book. The first word that I had to learn was O-X, ox. And there was the picture of the ox. It was quite a struggle.

As the years passed and it became time for first Eileen, then Maureen, to be taught to read, my parents found that I had already half done the job for them; I had taught my sisters to speak and write their alphabet. Relative to age, therefore, I was behind both of them, and not only in the matter of reading. I dawdled through my dressing, was always the last to be ready, was unable to tie my shoes, and Nanny had to get Eileen, two years younger, to do them for me.

When we went for walks I fell dreamily far behind, and Nanny wore herself out calling to me to catch up. One day I was startled as something poked me in my right eye. There were two moustached European gentlemen talking together, one of them was holding his walking-cane under his bent arm with the end pointed backwards, and I, in one of my usual brown studies, had walked my eye on to it.

I didn't know my right hand from my left. This was no small handicap when I did gym at a well known European school in Simla. At last I learnt that the left hand was on the side towards the wall-bars and the right towards the open door giving on to the playground, below which, and to the right, lay the football ground. At football we had to play shortened 'halves', due to the altitude of eight thousand feet. Otherwise, it was believed, one would strain one's heart. For many years afterwards, in order to tell my left hand from my right, I had mentally to transport my body back into that Simla gymnasium and arrange it with one arm towards the wall-bars and the other towards the open door.

Eileen was also able to tell the time before I could. Years later I was still being trained by my parents to tell it from the wall clock in the dining-room of our holiday abode Rock House, a converted corn store at which schooners used to unload, perched on the rocks at Sandy Cove near Kinsale. In a word, I was a late developer.

Other snatches of memory flick across the screen of my mind: walking along a dusty road and peering over a bridge across a dried-up stream, only to see a jackal and a snake intertwined in a fatal embrace, decomposing together in the torrid heat; a blazing copper sky arched over a flat world of sand and cacti that stretched to the horizon, towering eucalyptus trees, incredibly deep wells into which a child might drop a stone and then wait fascinated for a space of time before hearing the plop into water, the flocks of green parakeets flying into palm trees, below which the nannies sat gossiping, while the European children gathered round the bandstand listening to the Indian military musicians playing their European brass instruments, under the baton of a British army conductor; the pie-dogs from which one kept at a distance lest they had rabies, the fingerless lepers, the half-starved cattle with their ribs showing, the carriage drive to the shimmering waters and white marble causeways and pavilions of the gardens of Shalimar, the woman gathering up the cattle droppings from the roadway and patting them on to the outside of the walls of her mud house to dry for use as fuel, the temples and the mosques, the chorus of the jackals at night out in the mysterious moon-shadows of the cacti, sleeping with one's bed on the verandah or up on the flat roof, walking out in the garden on a milky night under a scented moon.

Since my father was in the Roads and Buildings branch of the P. W. D., roads and buildings had duly to be inspected. This meant much travelling. With each rise in rank the area to be inspected grew. When I was old enough to know, he was an Executive Engineer. Then he rose to the rank of Superintending Engineer with, I was told, responsibility for one third of the Punjab. Finally he was Chief Engineer of the Punjab and an *ex officio* member of the Punjab Government. At first it was a matter of our parents, amidst our wails, departing on a tour of inspection, and leaving us in the charge of Nanny. We were comforted by the comic picture postcards that they sent us.

Later I was old enough to accompany them, they on their horses, while I rode a pony, at least in theory. Actually, the pony rode me. The Indians had a habit, almost amounting to a nervous tic, of driving their animals by continually jerking at the reins, at the same time making clucking sounds with their tongues. The result was that my pony had developed a mouth like iron, impervious to any signals I might send along the reins. As for my using a curb, my mother banned this as cruel. So, if my pony decided that he wanted to leave the 'tan' (the specially prepared riding course along the side of the road) and make his way through the hedge on the non-road side, he made his way through the hedge, scratching my bare knees horribly. If he grew tired of my company, he threw me over his head. Always over his head. Never, just for once, sideways. My fall was not too hard, thanks to the softness of the tan and the solar topee (pith helmet) on my head. Nevertheless I gradually grew less fond of him, while he made no attempt to disguise his contempt for me.

I remember on one occasion, as we made our way through tea plantations, riding ahead of my parents singing hymns at the top of my voice. It wasn't that I 'had' religion; it was just that they were the only tunes that I knew. Anyhow I liked hymns. Every night, when they were home, my mother and father would come, separately, to kiss each of us goodnight and to sing each of us a verse or two of a hymn of our choosing. One hymn I shall never forget. It was at a missionary church that had been erected as cheaply as possible. A coat of whitewash on the upper surface of the corrugated iron roof alone mitigated the blast of the sun. The sweating congregation rose for the first hymn, only to find that they were being invited to sing, 'Summer Suns Are Glowing'. Well, that was true enough. The roof was almost incandescent. I think my pony had a religious streak; he never threw me while I was singing hymns. Perhaps he had been schooled by missionaries — a sort of Eurasian pony. Or perhaps he was aware that my father and mother were riding right behind him and that, if he took any liberties, they might sell him back to an Indian who would start tugging at his mouth again.

On these tours of inspection, our progress was sometimes mini-regal. First as a rule would ride my father and mother, he inspecting the road, she somehow managing to jot down the notes he barked out — 'pot-holes', 'metal collected' (i.e., the broken-up stone to be ground in by the steam-roller). I followed under the eyes of the bearer (chief servant) and the syce, who looked after the horses. The syce had married a wife of fourteen, and she was always giving trouble flirting with the other men in the servants' compound back at home. My father was frequently summoned to adjudicate. It was quite usual

14

for Europeans to be pressed into service as unofficial magistrates. Hindus were apt not to trust Moslem magistrates; nor Moslems, Hindus. Behind the syce rode the clerks, and finally, on foot, came coolies bearing the luggage. If we made our way through a village where white people seldom were seen, the whole village turned out to gaze. Once my foot came out of my stirrup. A dozen Indian children rushed forward to replace it for me.

Usually we spent the night in state rest-houses, but sometimes in tents. On one occasion we made our way up one of the five rivers of the Punjab, I forget which, in a house-boat. I was allowed to take over the wheel for a time. I began to steer away from the bank. The bearer seized the wheel from me only just in time to prevent my pulling the towing oxen into the river.

Because of the danger of thieves, my father slept with a Colt revolver under his pillow and my mother with some smaller form of revolver under hers. The thieves, to make themselves hard to catch, oiled their bodies, and even their loin-cloths were knotted so as to slip off easily. Once they took everything in a tent down to the bedclothes without waking my sisters. My father was a very heavy sleeper and my mother a very light one. An occasion arose when she couldn't be with him and he had to camp alone. What was to be done? He piled all the available furniture against the tent flap. Suddenly he awoke in the gloom to the sound of crashing. Seizing the Colt he rushed to the flap — and very nearly shot the bearer bringing in his shaving water.

My father was a sergeant in the Indian Defence Force, a force of European volunteers, engineers, doctors, civil servants, bankers, anyone. Of course the main burden of defence fell on the European-officered Indian Army, and on the British Army-in-India. World War One was raging in Europe at this time. My father had sought to enlist in the Indian Army, but European administrators could not be spared from the task of maintaining the British Raj. On one occasion I rode with him to watch him drilling. We were late. It was a relief therefore when we found the colonel, who had passed us in his car, broken down by the roadside. We hurried on. Again he passed us — and again broke down. In the end, my father was on the parade ground first.

In all the time that I was in India, including a later brief visit

15

between leaving my prep. school and going to my public school, I became aware, only as a child of course, of but two minor uprisings against the British, whereas attacks by Moslems on Hindus as they issued from their temples, or of Hindus on Moslems as they emerged from their mosques, were frequent. One such minor rising against the British occurred when we were staying with the European lady in charge of Queen Mary's College for Indian boys in Lahore, I think. I used to attend two classes a day, one in English spelling, and the other in Mathematics. I enjoyed the spelling lessons as I was, with the advantage of working in my mother tongue, the best, even being able to spell 'e-l-e-p-h-a-n-t'. In Mathematics the boys would be given sums in addition and subtraction. As each boy completed the sum, he would rush up to the teacher's desk with his slate to be marked. I couldn't compete (the boys in this class were older than I) and I finally slipped away and no longer attended.

The boys were upper class Moslems, Hindus and Sikhs. The Moslems and Hindus ate at separate tables. Where the Sikhs ate I can't remember. Perhaps, as a monotheistic Hindu sect, they ate with the Hindus. I at any rate took my food with the Moslems, who had no objection to sitting down with Christians. One day I found my self drafted into the position of being a judge as to which boy had the broadest thighs. Sikhs, Hindus and Moslems crowded round me, slapping the inside of their thighs and inviting my decision in their favour. In a land where wrestling was a highly regarded sport, physical strength was important.

One night my sisters and I were mysteriously roused from sleep and dressed. Evasive answers were given to all our questions. We were taken across the road to Queen Mary's College for Girls. The girls were upper class Indians and were in purdah. The Indian boys were taken across also but segregated in some building. All night long, as I learnt next day, Indian lancers patrolled up and down the road outside the walls. As I was European and only six, it was deemed safe to allow me, together of course with my sisters, to mingle with the girls, who had no need to cover their faces while within the school grounds. My father I learnt, as a sargeant in the Indian Defence Force, had donned khaki and gone off with his rifle and bayonet to command a road picket. Since the girls were in purdah and the school therefore had high walls, it had been chosen by the lancers as, of the two schools, the more defensible. I was, as something at least male, a centre of attraction to the girls. However, none of them came to any harm at my six-year-old hands. As I have said, I was a late developer.

Back again at Queen Mary's College for Boys, a number of the pupils informed me gleefully that my father had killed twenty men. That he was alleged to have slaughtered their own countrymen seemed to concern them not at all. They were ruling class Indians, even a rajah or two among them, and tended to identify with the British. On my father's return I examined him closely for signs of blood, but both his uniform and his hands appeared to be unstained.

My sisters and I hated the journey to The Hills. Whether we were zig-zagging our way up to Simla by the cog-railway from Kalka, or in our T-model Ford car, we were travel-sick. As the area of the Punjab which my father had to inspect grew, so did a car rather than horses become necessary. Before roads were taken over from the local Indian authorities to be 'metalled' and maintained in future by the P. W. D., my father had to vet them. Mere dust tracks, they were deeply pitted on each side by the passing of bullock-carts, the rims of whose wooden wheels were studded with broad-headed nails. The centre of the road was therefore in effect a mound which would scrape the bottom of a car that was not built with a good clearance. Hence the choice of the T-model Ford. American cars, with their big engines, hogged the Indian market. No inexpensive British car, with its engine kept small by the Home tax on horse-power, could have endured the long haul up to The Hills. In India the tax was assessed on the number of seats.

The T-model Ford had two levers up on the steering column, one to control the spark, the other the petrol. On the floor was a pedal. When the pedal was up the car was in high gear. When the pedal was in the mid position the driving belt slipped and the car was in neutral. When the pedal was down the car was in its only other gear, low. Low gear was immensely powerful but immensely slow. The lights worked directly off the engine, so that as the engine slowed the lights dimmed. How then, down in The Plains, to overtake a long herd of buffaloes, with their black skins and black eyes, being driven through a black Indian night? As we slowed down to creep past them, the lights dimmed and we could not see sufficiently. If we

17

increased the revolutions of the engine and so brought up the lights by going into low gear, the car was moving hardly any faster than the buffaloes. In the end my father used to succeed by a process of dodging to and fro between high and low gear.

Above the town of Simla, ringed by the giant snow-clad peaks of the Himalayas, was a clearing in the forests where the nurses and ayahs took the children. As we walked along towards it, on either side was the constant crashing of monkeys swinging from bough to bough. The monkeys evidently were near enough to us in physical and mental make-up to recognise an insult when it was offered. On one occasion we children, as the monkeys squatted in the branches around the clearing inspecting us, began to make faces at them. The monkeys almost at once exhibited signs of increasing anger by small menacing movements. Finally some of them descended from the trees and advanced on us. We scampered back to the safety of the nurses. Most of these, as distinct from Nanny, were wholly European.

On another occasion I heard bursts of laughter from a concealed road on a slightly lower level. Glancing over, I saw a number of ayahs in charge of European children. Three little boys were, no doubt necessarily, being assisted in the process of urination. But the ayahs had turned it into a competition as to who could achieve the greatest distance, like firemen practising throwing water with hoses. I turned away hurriedly from the shocking scene. Whatever would Nanny have said — Nanny, who would refer only to 'the bathroom' and to 'business'?

It was up in The Hills that I committed my first sin, heard my first joke, and had my first love affair.

The love affair was brief. It lasted in fact only for the length of a pony ride in Simla, plus its aftermath of memories. The lady, as young as myself, was the daughter of the Governor, Sir Edward McClagan. It was her ringlets that set my heart aflame. Those ringlets! I see them yet . . .

The joke was, 'If a bull ate a bomb, what would it be?' And the answer was, 'Abominable.' A — bomb — in — a — bull, see? But did I see? Not on your life. Three adults, my father, my mother, and the man who told the joke, wrestled for minutes on end trying to get the point home to me, their task rendered the harder by the fact that I didn't know the word 'abominable' in the first place.

There was also the shameful Episode of the Biscuits. My mother always kept on the sideboard a biscuit-container, the body of which was made of wood and shaped like a barrel, while the lid was of silver. The biscuits in the barrel happened to be of my favourite kind, sprinkled on top with sugar crystals. It must be added that my sisters and I had been strictly raised never to tell a lie. I had already had my tea in the nursery with Eileen and Maureen who were now in bed, while I, having reached the mature age of eight, was allowed to stay up later. The biscuit-barrel attracted me irresistibly. Finally I crept up to the sideboard, which was at chin height, raised my right arm, took off the lid and, plunging my left arm blindly into the barrel, groped around. At that moment Nanny entered the room. 'Are you taking biscuits?' she asked. 'No,' I replied, elbow-deep in them.

Later in bed, when my mother came to kiss me goodnight and sing me my chosen verse of a hymn, I confessed that I had lied to Nanny. 'I know, darling,' she said quietly, but no reproach followed. Charitably it was decided that I must be hungry and should in future be given supper. I was happy to go along with this theory, but in my heart of hearts I knew that it was just a case of a lust for biscuits sprinkled on top with sugar crystals.

My mother greatly prided herself on her rockcakes. These were always cooked and produced when, at Simla, she had some of the British troops in for afternoon tea and tennis. It was a common practice for Simla hostesses so to entertain the troops. The story is that one such hostess asked the soldiers, on their arrival, how they decided which of them was to come. 'We toss for it,' they said. 'Oh, I see, and you won!' 'No,' was the reply, 'we lost.'

In these nine years in India I never came across a snake, apart from the one decomposing with the jackal in a twin death inflicted on one another. Then, just before I was due to leave, I came across two. I was walking with my parents and the bearer through the pine woods at Dalhousie, I think. After all these years the Hill stations have become a blur in my mind — except Simla. Leopards were always about, and one was careful not to let one's dog out at night. Some neighbours who did so found, next morning, that traces of skin and bone were all that were left of their pet. Suddenly I lost my footing and found myself at the bottom of a small ravine in the company of a large snake. The next moment I was aware of Therarb, in his bearer's uniform and puggery (turban), bounding down the bank and hauling me up to safety. Subsequent enquiries conducted by my parents established that the snake was dead; it had been killed by the servants the day before up on our roof, and the carcass had been thrown down into the ravine.

Therarb was a mixture of the old and the new. I remember his once taking my sisters and me into his room in the servants' compound and showing us his set of crudely coloured pictures of the ancient Hindu gods, and the next moment his brand new European safety razor (the other men seemed to use what appeared to me as a child to be a sharpened bone or some such). Therarb's face was heavily pockmarked from smallpox. After I had left India I heard that he had, a most unusual thing, contracted the disease for a second time; and that this time he had died of it.

The second snake was definitely at Dalhousie. We were mostly on foot, but we three children were taking turns to ride our Hill Pony. These Hill ponies were never shod and were almost as sure-footed and active as the leopards. The pony became more and more restive, we couldn't tell why. On rounding a corner we saw a snake lying across our path. My father knocked it out, pounding it with his khud stick (a long stave, tipped with a metal point, useful for climbing). He then placed stones on top of the whole length of the reptile, explaining that snakes were extremely hard to kill. We proceeded on to picnic and bathe at Panch Pul (the place of five pools, 'panch' meaning 'five'). On our return the snake had gone, though the stones still lay across the mountain track in disarray.

My best friend was Michael. For Michael and myself a 'walk' consisted of an almost non-stop wrestling match. One day he paused in the wrestling, regarded my shoes fixedly, and then with round serious eyes turned to my parents and his. 'Why,' he demanded, 'are Dorman's laces always undone?' No one seemed able to furnish him with an answer. I suppose the answer was that Eileen couldn't always be present to tie them up for me; or, to put it in a more all-embracing way, that I was a late developer. It wouldn't make a bad epitaph, really. If anyone can be bothered to put up a memorial to me, perhaps they will inscribe on it, 'Why were Dorman's laces always undone?'

Chapter Two
Simla & The Hills

The time came to go Home. The First World War had been over a year, travel was becoming easier, and I was nine and should have been in a 'proper' prep. school before this. It was held by my parents that, for their health's sake, European children should not stay out in India after the age of seven. It was also held that the few small European day schools around were adequate only for the beginning stages.

We travelled across the desert to Karachi by train. We children had never seen the sea, a ship, a poor European, or a domestic pig. These wonders now lay before us. There was then no air-conditioning, so a huge block of ice in an open-work crate stood in the middle of the carriage. On top of it was placed our milk and butter. In the vast spaces of India, railway journeys lasted days and nights, so the carriages were large, the seats padded for sleeping on, and there were pull-out berths suspended at their outer edge by chains from the ceiling. Both berths and seats ran along the length of the carriage, and not across its width as at Home. There was no corridor, and each carriage had its own toilet facilities. The dining-car was reached, and returned from, by the train's stopping and the passengers' descending on to the track side.

As we crossed the desert, the ice slowly melted, sending streams of water across the floor. The woodwork of the window-sills became so hot that we could not touch it. All, that is, except my father. He sat close to a window with a fly-swat. It was a normal activity to swat flies; one could become very skilful. Suddenly my mother said, 'What *are* you doing, Stew?' His proper name was Stewart. We saw that he was neatly decapitating the corpses of the flies with his penknife. In response to my mother's implied protest, he abandoned his gruesome task. Before the reader begins to weave freudian explanations too glibly, I might mention that, when later fishing for mackerel in Ireland, he always broke the backs of the fish, as each one was caught, just behind the head. He wished to save them from a slow death in the bottom of the boat. Doubtless he equally wished to make certain that each fly was truly dead.

We sailed on the 'City of London'. As we approached the Suez Canal, the pulsations of our engines became noticeably more urgent. The word went round that the captain was trying to get to the Canal before a faster sister ship, the 'City of Berlin'. The 'City of Berlin', taken over we were told from the Germans as a part of war reparations and renamed, had proved rather too large for the Canal on her previous trip. (The Canal had not then been dredged to its present depth.) She had stuck, being freed only after a considerable delay to herself and other shipping. Our captain didn't wish to risk being involved in a similar hold-up. Daily we looked astern, but could see nothing. Daily we looked at the passenger's notice-board where our run was recorded on a map showing our course to Britain. The days' runs became longer in response to the pounding of the engines. Finally, as we entered the mouth of the Canal, we saw the menacing shape of the 'City of Berlin' on the horizon. But we were safe.

On leaving Port Said and entering Mediterranean climes, it was deemed no longer necessary to wear our solar topees. Those adults not returning to India, and all the children, tossed theirs overboard. We watched the flotilla of light pith boats bobbing and dropping astern. Some had been furnished by their owners with masts and sails.

At Aden we mounted the island in a taxi to see the ancient tanks hewn out of the rock. Almost naked little boys stood begging. 'No farder, no mudder,' they chanted, and this was followed by an explanatory double slap on their apparently empty bellies. The chant went on and on. 'No farder, no mudder,' slap slap, slap slap. 'No farder, no mudder,' slap slap, slap slap . . . They appeared to have come into the world by spontaneous generation. Anyhow it worked; the coins showered on them.

All the European children on the boat spoke, naturally, both

Hindustani and English. All the European children in the world spoke, surely, both Hindustani and English? But no. There was one boy, the son we were told of the Bishop of Bombay, who *spoke only Hindustani*! Fancy that! A European boy of seven or eight who couldn't speak English! We gazed at the monstrosity in a kind of awe. At Marseilles a man came on board selling balloons filled, not with air like ordinary toy balloons, but with gas. When you held the string, the balloon floated straight up. We asked our mother to buy us one each, but she said that they were too expensive. The son of the Bishop of Bombay was bought a balloon. Almost at once he let go the string and the balloon soared away over the mastheads. He set up a howl. Fancy letting go the string of an expensive balloon! But then, what else could one expect of a boy who could speak only Hindustani?

After I had been installed in my prep. school, Castle Park at Dalkey in County Dublin (Dalkey has since become absorbed into Greater Dublin), my parents returned to India with my sisters. But later my sisters too were brought back and put into a boarding-school, Hillcourt in neighbouring Glenageary. Hillcourt was a sister school to Castle Park. When my time there was completed, I was taken to London by my Uncle Tom, shown the lights of Piccadilly Circus, and placed on board a liner under the nominal control of a lady missionary. But as the liner was small, merely under ballast and therefore light and easily tossed around by a sea that proved not really calm even in the Mediterranean, even in the Red Sea, even in the Indian Ocean; and as the missionary was a bad sailor, I scarcely saw her throughout the voyage.

When we called in at Algiers I went ashore alone, though I never strayed too far from the other passengers. The first thing of interest that I saw were two Algerians fighting. Fezes on their heads and dressed in loose white garments, they gripped one another with both hands by the shoulders and went round and round in an anti-clockwise direction, kicking one another in the bottom and shouting at one another in Arabic. I followed the passengers into the fruit and vegetable market. There was a very popular song at the time which went:

Yes, we have no bananas,
We have no bananas today.

French- and Arabic-speaking Algiers apparently had heard of it for, doubtless for our benefit and that of other English-speaking tourists, banners were stretched across the market ways reading, 'Yes, we have no bananas' — of which of course there were mountains. Every time I perused one of these banners, I was conscious of gleaming smiles of delight on dusky Arab faces.

After three weeks on an unstable sea, Bombay appeared to be equally unstable and pitching about for an hour or two. I found that I had forogtten most of my Urdu (Hindustani). It was frustrating to hear my father and mother talking fluently, while I remained cut off from the crowds on the quay. When I had been in India previously I had scarcely given a thought to snakes, but now I seemed to hear them in every hiss and every rustle. When I went to bed I took a stick in with me under my mosquito-net.

We travelled up to Ambala in the Punjab. Ambala was in The Plains and it was fiery hot. When on one occasion my mother asked me, around noon, to pick her some flowers in the garden, I drew a blanket round myself to keep the heat *out*. We slept out on the verandah. Because of no cloud or vapour cover, the temperature drops enormously in the night. For that reason we children, when very young, had worn 'binders' in bed, a ring of wool as wide as a scarf around our tummies to prevent our catching a chill. I was now deemed too old for a binder. But my mother insisted that I sleep with at least the sheet over me, even though my sweating limbs were sticking together or to my body. To make sleep even more difficult, the garden was filled with the harsh cries of peacocks, surely one of the ugliest sounds in the world! That obscure humorist, Nature, striking a balance against the extreme beauty of their plumage?

It was a relief when we cycled off at five in the morning to play golf. Putting was extremely difficult. The 'greens' were no more than rollered patches of parched earth on which the ball ran on and on as upon a billiard table. By seven the heat was building up and we returned home. On the first occasion, for some reason, I set off for home ahead of my parents but lost my way. Having forgotten most of my Urdu, I couldn't ask it. At that early hour we had come out not wearing our topees. The sun was rapidly gaining strength. Brought up in the belief that, without a topee, one could become severely ill with sunstroke and even possibly die, I grew more and more panic-stricken. Suddenly I caught sight of our house.

In later years my mother told me that fewer and fewer people were bothering with topees. The belief was growing that sunstroke was inflicted mainly through the eyes, and they contented themselves with dark glasses and a light head covering that shaded the backs of their necks. Certainly I wore the darkest glasses, with side pieces, that we could find. Nevertheless, after driving (there were no driving licences and the roads were mostly empty) for an hour, I usually had a headache. But then, as discovered later when I was given spectacles, I had unsuspected myopia and astigmatism.

One day my father raced the car full out from one milestone to the next. We timed ourselves as there was no speedometer. We clocked twenty-eight miles an hour. The roads were marked with milestones and smaller furlong stones. On one occasion my father pointed out to me stone towers rising above the trees of a jungle. They had been placed there by a rajah to act as milestones, when he and his entourage hunted tigers from the backs of elephants.

Eventually we left the furnace of Ambala for Simla and The Hills. The T-Model Ford zig-zagged the endless miles up. When we unscrewed the radiator cap to replenish the water, steam burst out. The road was barely wide enough to allow two vehicles to pass. On one side the khud rose almost sheer and on the other side fell away almost sheer. Only a low parapet made of loose stones stood between us and the drop. At frequent intervals the parapet had a gap in it to allow, in the deluge of the monsoons, the water to escape. Otherwise the parapet would have carried away. At two places we passed a rough wooden cross to mark where a European rider and his horse had gone over.

After a night spent in a rest-house, we continued. We had mounted most of the eight thousand feet up to Simla, when we saw a hillman. He began to run in front of the car, the whites of his eyes rolling as he glanced back in terror, like some farm animal at Home. If we slowed up and called to him to stand to one side, he merely slackened his pace and took a breather. If we speeded up in the hope of forcing him, through sheer exhaustion, to stand on one side, we merely increased his terror and he his pace. On and on he ran, always of course uphill, and with an incredible stamina. We were at our wits'

25

end when suddenly, again just like an animal, he saw a less steep place and burst up the side of the khud. My father said that because of inbreeding there were a more than average number of imbeciles among the Hillmen.

We had the opposite experience a few hours later. With a total stupidity on such a road, a car came round a corner far too fast. My father had to run us into the stone wall lining the inner side, damaging a mudguard. The other motorist, lucky not to go over the khud, sped on. At that moment the wild-looking head of a hillman appeared out of a bush above us. With all the sophistication of London's Regent Street, and in very passable English, he shouted out, 'Take his number!'

I had never been higher than the eight thousand feet of Simla, but now my parents took me further up the Himalayas, my memory is to nine or ten thousand feet. I can't remember any place names. We went on horseback. When I asked why, they told me that no one except the Viceroy, the Commander-in-Chief, and the Maharajah of Somewhere-or-Other, was allowed to drive a car above Simla, because if the danger to riders.

One day we rode through continuous snow. The shod horses of my parents hobbled along, the snow gathering itself up into a hard ball in the cup formed by the curve of their hoof plus the horseshoe, and pressing against the quick of their feet. There were constant pauses while the snow was scooped out by our syce. My hill pony, being unshod, was quite unaffected. As we rode higher and higher the language gradually changed, more and more local folk words or pronunciations coming in. Finally, when asking the way, my parents could no longer make themselves understood, and even the servants had the greatest difficulty. We hired guides to lead the horses. The cold became so intense and the snowing so miserable that I found myself blubbering and quite unable to stop. The hillman leading my pony seemed to be one of those imbeciles that my father had spoken about, for he regarded my blubbering features with a non-stop stare and a meaningless grin on his face.

Finally we reached the state rest-house (dak bungalow). A huge scented fire of fir cones and pine logs dripping resin blazed a welcome. The main part of our baggage was following behind us, carried by a string of coolies. As the snow continued to fall, we quite gave up all hope of seeing it that day. How could the men make their way after dark through the deep rifts? They would certainly stop somewhere for the night. But miraculously, some hours later, there they were! 'Shah barsh' — I continue to spell words as I pronounced them — 'well done!' said my father as he paid them off, with a bonus as 'buck sheesh'.

The face of the Scotsman with whom we had joined up on the journey darkened. He wore a kilt and had a wicked-looking dirk in his stocking. *His* coolies had set out at the same time as ours, and *his* coolies hadn't arrived. He left the room. Apparently my parents knew him from before, for my mother said with a worried look, 'Oh dear, I hate this! I know there's going to be trouble; he's a very bad-tempered man.'

The next day the sun shone on deep crisp snow. I had had such a bad time the day before, that my father had the greatest difficulty in persuading me that it was warm enough to emerge from the rest-house and make a snowman, his mouth, nose and eyes formed from pieces of charcoal. But he was right. The combination of sharp mountain air and a blazing sun was wonderful. The wonder was spoilt by the sound of bellowing. The Scotsman's coolies had arrived. They stood in a line with bowed shoulders while he prowled up and down before them shouting his fury. I almost expected to see the dirk plucked from his stocking and lodged in the chest of one of them. At last the ugly scene was over, he paid them off, and they slunk away.

The rajah of the small state of Mundi — I hope I have spelt it right; to me as a boy the sound of its name merely suggested the word 'Monday' — was only, I was told, still a pupil at Queen Mary's College in Lahore. The state was being governed during his minority by a British regent who was a friend of my parents. No car ever ventured along the hair-raising single-track mountain road except that driven by the rajah's chauffeur. In this we travelled round hairpin bends, on our left the khud hurling itself up to the sky, on our right plunging down to distant valleys. As we arrived, we passed a fair. I longed to join the crowds, but my parents wouldn't allow it because of the likely presence of lepers.

Next day we joined the regent on a lofty, gorgeously decorated, and covered dais. Servants stood behind us waving fans on the ends

27

of poles. The procession of the gods and goddesses passed below along the crowd-lined roadway. Each god was an effigy clothed in splendid garments carried on two poles borne on the shoulders of four men, two in front and two behind. As they passed before the dais each diety acknowledged the presence of the rajah, represented by the regent, by the bearers making the god bob up and down.

The state had been suffering a drought. A palace official saw us back to the state guest-house, the regent having an engagement to punish the rain god by placing him in the river. There the stone image would remain until rain appeared. Not a bad idea, really! Imagine putting statuettes of God the Father, God the Son and God the Holy Ghost into the fountains in Trafalgar Square in London until, say, the rate of inflation came down! Instead of bowing and kneeling and crawling and snivelling before our gods, treat 'em rough, say I!

As we drove away from The Hills to return to The Plains, prior to sailing for Home, the last sound that I took with me was that of the voice of a little Gurkha sergeant drilling his men, 'Lep wight, lep wight, lep wight . . .'

At Amritsar we viewed the Golden Temple of the Sikhs, an Indian policeman standing behind us to guard us. We viewed the government buildings of New Delhi, blindingly whitewashed in the sun. We watched a military tattoo in Delhi Fort, the galloping British horsemen towing their guns in patterned near-collisions that never became absolute, the beams of the searchlights, probing the sky, cut short because of the absence of any clouds or water vapour for them to shine on.

At Agra Fort we peered into the semi-precious stone set in the wall which precisely reflected the Taj Mahal some distance away. But when we came back again next day, my father was not allowed to keep his walking-stick nor my mother her sunshade. Some American tourists had been round the Fort, and after they left the stone had been discovered missing, prised from its setting by a souvenir-hunter. However, another stone set elsewhere into the marble had been found that was almost as good, and we viewed the Taj in that.

Next day we visited the Taj Mahal itself in the afternoon, then later returned to see it by moonlight. The Americans were there. They were singing some sentimental song to the full moon, all wearing their topees. I viewed them contemptuously with uncharitable fourteen-year-old eyes; whoever heard of anyone wearing a topee at night! As we walked up to the Taj, the intense brilliance of moonlight travelling through a vapourless sky, and reflected off the white marble, set up an effulgence that gave me the sensation of not being quite sure when I had actually reached the face of the building. I even stretched out my hand and touched it to reassure myself.

We returned to the gate and mounted the steps leading to the top. The gates to such monuments are considerable buildings in themselves. My father set up his camera on the parapet. He focused it on the Taj and left it there with the shutter open to give the plate a one-hour exposure. No fast film then! We spread out a picnic in the limpid night. Next morning the development of the plate revealed the moonlight photograph to be a total failure. Yet postcards bearing pictures of the Taj by moonlight were freely on sale in Agra. As we were leaving that day for Bombay and Home, and my father had promised me a moonlight Taj for my picture-postcard collection, he bought one from an Indian street vendor. How had the latter managed to obtain it? The vendor was astoundingly frank. 'Oh,' he said, 'I take it in daylight through smoked glass.'

We sailed from Bombay in an Italian liner. In the Mediterranean we met a sister ship. When one British ship passes another, each sedately dips its ensign. But when one Italian liner meets another, each sheers up almost alongside as if it were a racing yacht, and there is shouting and waving. We sailed up the main 'street' of Venice, desembarked, and were transferred in a gondola by narrow canals to our *pensione*. I developed a fetish for going up towers. I looked up in the guide book every tower and dome of over two hundred and fifty feet or so, and panted my way up them in Venice, Verona, Milan, Rome. My father willingly accompanied me. A roads and buildings engineer, he was used to ascending ladders and scaffolding to inspect work. Then it was to Stresa in the mountainous north of Italy, to Lausanne in Switzerland, and to Paris and a production in a French translation of Shaw's 'Saint Joan'.

Back in Ireland, as I stood in my gown (like our sister public school Radley in England we wore gowns) in the cloisters of St. Columba's College awaiting the chapel bell, an under-sized and stupid-looking senior boy came up to me. 'Are you a new boy?' he demanded. 'Yes,' I said with a smile that was intended to be disarming, and huddling a little closer to the other new boys. 'Well, don't give me any of your guff!' As I had not given him guff, cheek, impertinence, or anything else except a smile, I was at a loss. Thinking that he had departed, I turned to the others. 'What did I do?' I was conscious of an agonising pain. He was standing behind me, having just given me a savage kick exactly in the anus.

As the term wore on, I was to learn that this was his speciality; to move up silently behind a younger boy and, for no immediate reason whatever, deliver his kick. He never missed the target. Nature having given him neither brains nor physique nor looks, I suppose that this was the only way he had of asserting himself. Some people develop into boxing champions, some into advanced electronic engineers, some write symphonies, some become prime ministers, and some go around kicking other people in the anus. It's as simple as that. It was a relief nevertheless when, for some reason or other, he left at the end of the term. Perhaps, in a moment of absent-mindedness, he had kicked the headmaster in the anus.

I had not then the enthusiasm for increasing my knowledge of French that I have since acquired. Mr. Lewis, a Welshman, was our French master. After an exhausting struggle on his part to develop my grasp of irregular verbs, he would exclaim, adapting the advertisement of a well-known brand of soapflakes, 'You're like Lux, Dorman — a little of you goes a long way.' He was a dashing man, it being rumoured among us that he had come near to winning a Welsh rugby cap. He also drove fast in fast cars. It was his theory that the safest way to negotiate a road crossing was at full speed. One day he was involved in a collision. On his emergence from hospital, a number of the school staff said to him, 'Now what about your theory?' 'Well man,' he replied, 'if I'd been travelling faster he wouldn't have got me.'

There is a considerable truth in this. The greater the velocity, the less time spent at the likely point of collision. If, as car engines improved, the minimum permitted speed on the highway was set at, say, a hundred and fifty miles an hour, not only would the chances of a crossroads collision between two vehicles become more remote, but also, should such a collision occur, death almost certainly would be instantaneous and there would be no suffering. This leaves one matter unresolved. The community's disposal services would still be burdened with the task of removing the bodies and vehicles. But if, with a yet further improvement in engine design, the minimum speed were lifted to, for the sake of argument, a quarter of the speed of light, this should ensure that both bodies and vehicles were vaporised. How would one commemorate the deceased? Well, when someone is buried at sea, one drops a wreath on the waters. If someone is vaporised, one attaches the wreath to a balloon. Also, such a velocity should help to prevent a collision where there was a stream of traffic approaching the crossing, as opposed to a single vehicle. But shopping would be difficult.

Speaking of collisions, I was involved in one myself. My Uncle Tom and Aunt Ethel were now farming up in the Dublin mountains at Glencullen. Thither I made my way on a bicycle by mountain tracks on Sundays, with a school 'exeat' in my pocket. As well as our Sunday suits, we were expected to wear bowler hats. Imagine the misery of riding past a lot of irreverent village boys with a bowler hat on your head! I resolved the difficulty by swapping my brand new and expensive hat with a boy who had one which had become so fatigued with age and ill-use, that it could be completely concertinaed down. Thus I rode out of the school gate in full Sunday gear, but no sooner had I reached the highroad than I compressed the bowler into a flat disk-like object which I clutched as I rode along. In the unlikely event of my meeting a member of the staff, it could be instantly reinflated.

The return trip took the form of an almost continuous and glorious gently-downhill evening rush past gorse and heather and through hamlets, with scarcely a turn of the pedals necessary. The final approach to the school was down a long steep hill, and it was a matter of religion and conscience among us boys that the descent should be accomplished without the application of brakes. I, being less than heroic, sneaked the odd touch on mine. I daresay others did the same. On this occasion the boy whom I had taken home with me, doubtless having sneaked rather fewer touches, was ahead. In the gloaming a horse and cart appeared. I saw its silhouette clearly enough but, my short-sightedness having increased since my glasses were fitted, I judged it to be going away from me whereas it was approaching. My time and my position judgments for avoiding it were thus both put out of joint. The next moment I was flung on to the road as I hurtled into the horse's chest. I was conscious of the horse's rearing up above me, of my friend, who had stopped and come back, peering anxiously at me; of the driver's voice (we were out of sight of each other) calling out, 'Is he dead? Is he dead?'; and of myself, though much shaken, concerned mainly with inspecting my bicycle. I straightened the handlebars, and all was well.

At a later date my parents had a house at Crosshaven in County Cork. One day a man on a motor-bike ran into a horse and cart close to the nearby village of Carrigaline. A shaft entered his chest, impaling him. Those who came to assist had the gruesome task of prising the body off. I not only had missed the shafts, but also the bony shoulders of the horse, exactly striking the soft muscles of its chest. In all this concern on the part of the other two for me, and I for my bicycle, the poor horse got forgotten. Imagine how you would feel if you were plodding along lawfully between your shafts, doing the job you were fed to do, when suddenly an ape-like creature with its body covered in bits of cloth, balancing on top of a metal contraption, hurtled into your chest! I bet you'd rear up. I certainly would.

At breakfast time, seven thirty as I remember, the master on duty used to stand at the door of the dining-hall. Behind the High Table at the end of the long hall were stained-glass windows. The master inspected our dress and general state of tidiness as we entered. If we were late, we were put on Penal Drill. Penal Drill took the form of the Sergeant's making us hop round and round a semi-quadrangle on one leg, and other similar tortures. I was quite often booked for Penal Drill.

Then a boy, one of a small and daring band, taught me how to get out of bed only at the very last of the warning bells, take a hot and a cold bath, dry and dress, and yet never be late. As the bell went one leapt out, hurled off one's pyjamas, seized a towel and ran naked down the corridor, jumped into the turgid waters of the hot bath that already had had many bodies in it (the school is now equipped with showers), thence straight into the cold bath (only a cissy didn't take a cold bath), back naked down the corridor drying in the rush of air and the odd rub of the towel, vest on, shirt with the tie already arranged and knotted in the collar, but left in a circle wide enough to admit the head, pulled on; slip-knot of the tie drawn tight up to the gullet, step straight into one's pants and trousers which had been arranged the night before on the floor beside the bed one inside the other to form a double ring, pull them up, socks and elastic-sided slippers on, gown held in teeth and jacket pulled on as one rushed down the corridor, gown on as one crossed the Big Schoolroom and descended the staircase into the main quadrangle, every third fly-button fastened as one hurtled across the quad, every second shirt button done up as one crossed the end of the cloisters, gown drawn tightly around one to hold the whole ramshackle arrangement together as one approached the master on duty, panting suppressed and his probing eye warded off with a demure and civil good-morning, dressing completed at the table during the reciting of the Latin grace. Penal Drill! What's Penal Drill? Never heard of it.

When the time came for us to be Confirmed, this was done in the college chapel by the Archbishop of Dublin. As he stood by the altar rails, we knelt down before him two by two. He put a hand on each of our heads, our hair greased down with a green concoction in gold-coloured tins which we bought in Dublin at Woolworth's. It was called 'Solidified Hair Dressing'. I always got the word wrong and called it 'Solified'. I had then a genius for getting words and phrases wrong. I used to wish people on their birthdays, 'Many re-happy turns of the day.'

But of course we had to be prepared for the ceremony. Sex and religion always seem to go together. Therefore, although the then Warden (headmaster) answered a few earnest questions about the interpretation of some biblical passage or other, the theme of masturbation held the centre of the stage. Each candidate went one by one to the study to be interviewed. I was a sensitive youth. I think the Warden perceived the intensity of my shrinking from the embarrassment to come, for all he said, looking at me significently, was, 'I think you are a boy who *thinks*.' So my thoughtfulness saved me. (Couldn't one masturbate thoughtfully?)

But it wasn't so with the late Geoffrey Witherington. I wasn't aware of his existence at the time I was at St. Columba's College, he being a mere New Boy, in other words, an Untouchable. But he was very much aware of me, I being one of the Lords of the Sixth

Form. We met years later, at a school in Kent where he was teaching English and I French and German. I had been but an undistinguished member of the college rugby first fifteen, but he had later become no less than captain, with in addition a Leinster Schoolboy Trial match to his credit — in short, a tough rugby type. The Warden had no doubts, when it came to the interview, where he stood with him. 'Which do you want to be, Witherington, a bullock or a bull?' Young Witherington, perceiving the required answer, replied stoutly, 'A bull, sir.' The Warden gathered his forces. In his heartiest man-to-man no-beating-about-the-bush manner, he came straight out with it. 'DON'T MASTURBATE, WITHERINGTON!'

Just before I left St. Columba's College, Uncle Lennox Robinson escorted my sisters and myself to meet our parents, returning from India on an Italian liner due to dock at Naples. After the meeting, Uncle Lennox left us for Capri, while we toured Naples, Pompeii, Florence, Rome. I had been reading George Eliot's *Savonarola* (nearly every penny of my pocket money at this time went on buying all the novels of Jane Austen, Dickens, Thackeray, George Eliot, the Brontes and the other Victorians) and for me Florence was bathed in a saffron glow of romance. Everywhere I saw Savonarola, Dante, Beatrice, Leonardo da Vinci. In Rome, with all the enormous self-consciousness of seventeen, I felt embarrassed wearing my school clothes and above all my schoolboy cap, over-topping as I did most of the not-very-tall male adult inhabitants. I had almost reached my ultimate six feet. Coming from temperate Ireland, I felt physically comfortable only when we entered the cool of some gallery, whereas my mother, straight from the fires of an Indian sun, put on her coat. Out in the sun- drenched streets my parents were in their element, whereas I had to be left behind in the hotel one day with a headache.

It wasn't only in the matter of acclimatisation that I differed from my father. Catologue in hand he would 'do' each gallery picture by picture, showcase by showcase, whereas I was given to sitting for ten minutes before a single statue, standing for five minutes before a single picture, and totally ignoring all showcases. I'm not much taken with the minutiae of life; I like the large strong effect. I'm not a pottery and jewellery man; I'm more a cathedral man. 'Human' stories in newspapers seldom attract my attention. I prefer a wholsesale slaughter to your single private domestic killing — the big canvas, the large effect. Murder and pottery are not much in my line; it's cathedrals and massacres that arouse my enthusiasm. Watercolours make me yawn; give me every time a great hairy chap sloshing on oil paint with a pallet knife. Give me old Michaelangelo or Rubens splashing the paint around and covering half a wall or most of the ceiling. I find a small Henry Moore tedious. But let him get his teeth into a thirty-ton boulder and I'm with him all the way.

Chapter Three
Recollections of Oxford College Life

As I approached Oxford by train at the beginning of the Michaelmas Term in the year 1930, I was, like the majority of Freshmen, just a green schoolboy of, in my case, nineteen — but not quite green enough for the railway sharks. And what a feast for the sharks it was! Thousands of very young men, hopefully with more money than sense, swarming down on Oxford all within a day or two.

We had just stopped at a station, when the man in the bowler hat got in. I was alone in the compartment. My two heavy suitcases were up on the luggage rack. I was well dressed, except for a pair of shabby brown shoes. Friendly fashion, the Bowler Hat engaged me in conversation. But he kept glancing at those shoes. Plainly they caused him unease. Was I up on a scholarship? No, I was paying fees in the ordinary way. We stopped at the next station. He got out on to the platform, but kept the carriage door open. He looked up and down the platform. I saw him raise his arm in a signal.

It dawned upon me then that the questions he had rained down on me all served but a single purpose; to establish whether I had money. I left the compartment. I made my way up the corridor to a cousin who I knew was travelling on his honeymoon. I hated to intrude, but my alarm was considerable. Kindly he came back with me. The entire compartment, except for my seat in the far corner by the window, was now filled by hard-faced bowler-hatted men. In a complete silence, my cousin and I each took a suitcase from the rack and walked out. What precise form of misery I had escaped, I do not know. Violent robbery, seeing the greatness of the forces that had been marshalled against me? Perhaps not. There was far less violent crime then than now. Some card-sharping?

I took a taxi to Worcester College, and found that it was close to the station. I entered in awe and excitement through the lofty portal. To the right, behind a counter, stood a man with a formidable beard. Though the rest of him also was large enough to have swallowed me up, he addressed me throughout as 'sir'. Later I learnt that his name was Buller. Also that he was, together with the Dean, the discipline in the College. One afternoon, after being at a tea-party in nearby Walton Street, I entered the Gatehouse with my face made up in a variety of colours. Why? Just a bit of schoolboy silliness and high spirits. But I remember feeling very firmly that I had the right to do so; it contravened no college rule. The immense man did not roar. Just a deprecatory smile parted his moustache from his beard. 'It's not the *thing*, sir.' No fist, descending from on high, could have crushed me more completely than that little smile.

Having dragged my two suitcases up the stairs to nearly the top of the tallest building in Worcester, and distributed my things about my sitting-room and bedroom, I descended to attend the Provost at his lodgings close by. Dr Lys appeared to me as a frail man. He asked me if I knew Sorrento in Italy. Seeing me, a schoolboy used to being examined, knitting my brow, he hastened to assure me that I was no longer under examination.

'It's only,' he said, 'that you've spelt your Uncle Lennox Robinson's address on your form as *Sorento Cottage* — with one r.'

My uncle and godfather, the late Dr Lennox Robinson, was, as said before, a co-director with Lady Gregory, W B Yeats and others of the Irish National Theatre, the Abbey Theatre. Being the family's man-of-the-world, what with the performance and publication of his plays in London, New York and Dublin, he had been put in charge by my parents in India of seeing me into Oxford. This task he performed on a comparatively lavish scale, buying me, for instance, four hats, although I never wore a hat; and a dozen white waistcoats to wear with my 'tails', bought later, though two or three would have been enough.

Defensive about my spelling, I continued to maintain to Dr Lys that Sorrento Cottage had one r — absurdly, of course. When I passed my Responsions into Oxford, the examiner at my *viva voce* said that he had made a list of my spelling mistakes that extended half way down the page. Later, on coming down from Oxford and setting up as a free-lance in Chelsea, writing articles for some twenty British and Irish periodicals, and ghosting some half dozen books for the London publishers Putnam and Company, I determined never to send out a piece with a single spelling mistake in it. Even if I had only a half per cent doubt, I looked up a word. As a result of this I knocked my spelling, if not into perfection, at least into shape.

But to return to college discipline. Shortly after we Freshmen arrived at Worcester, we were summoned to assemble in Hall. There the Dean, Colonel Wilkinson, quite as tall and even more imposing than Buller, Porter (Keeper-of-the-Gate), addressed us on the subject of what was acceptable behaviour and what was not. (Most of us at my public school in the Dublin mountains, St Columba's College, a sister school of Radley, went to Dublin University, but that year three of us came up to Oxford, myself to Worcester, the late Robert Talbot to Keble, and the late Nicholas Mansergh, afterwards Dr Nicholas, Master of St John's College, Cambridge, to Pembroke.) With the sweeping simplifications of youth, the word being put about was that Colonel Wilkinson was a wealthy man whose house somewhere in the country boasted a cellar of fine spirits and wines. Also that he was a bachelor. These two facts, it was alleged, influenced his judgements. Should you find yourself up before him on a matter of drunkenness, he would survey the charge with a lenient eye, doubtless as a misdemeanour only to be expected occasionally from a properly constituted young blood. But if the charge involved some contretemps with a woman, his reaction would be merciless.

A staircase close to the lodgings of Dr Lys, the Provost, ascended to my top storey rooms. From there I was able to look down on to the quadrangle. I was also able to hear Colonel Wilkinson, leaning on his walking-stick, laying bets with a group of particularly self possessed freshmen that they couldn't run twice round the quad before he could walk round it once. At the time, I regarded this group as a snobbish clique. In hindsight, unfairly. They were merely mostly from St Paul's school, naturally knew one another already, and their numbers gave them confidence. They also gave Worcester College one of its best oarsmen. Rowing at stroke, he took the Torpid crew into five successive 'bumps', and on the sixth day covered the course as Head of the River so fast, that the crew behind was left almost out of sight.

The newspapers had been full of reports of Britain's wonderful new dirigible, the R-100. One day, shaving in my lofty bedroom, I looked up to find the view from my window filled by an enormous nose, with 'R-100' written across it in gigantic characters. The airship, hydrogen-filled like her sister ship the R-101, and dismantled when the latter crashed with forty-seven deaths, was gliding over Oxford at little more than roof height.

A Portuguese student across the landing from me had bottles of unmatured port sent to him by his father, a wine merchant in Oporto. He gave me a couple of bottles. I once saw a list of drinks arranged in the order of their alcoholic content. Port headed the list of wines as having the most. One summer day, parched with thirst, I hastened in from a tennis match to dress for a Latin tutorial with Mr. A. N. Bryan-Brown. Regarding the unmatured port as merely a fruit-juice drink, I filled a tumbler to the brim and gulped the lot down on an empty stomach. Suddenly, sitting elbow to elbow with Mr. Bryan-Brown as he patiently and courteously exposed to me the horrors of my written work, my head began to swim. Then my speech became slurred. Finally it deserted me altogether. I sat there, sweating. My only hope was that, my Latin being so appalling, he would regard my frozen silence as merely an outstanding example of sub-human ignorance. Just as all seemed lost (I doubted my ability even to rise from my seat and get out of the room) my head cleared as suddenly as it had clouded over, and I successfully staggered my uncertain course to the end of the tutorial.

Before coming to Worcester College, I had never partaken of any alcoholic drink. At the college there was a heavy, though largely unspoken, pressure on one to imbibe. So a little beer, unwillingly, I drank in Hall. One day my friend from school days, Robert Talbot of Keble College, proposed to take me on a pub crawl. I was given to understand that undergraduates were not allowed to visit pubs. Two Proctors, assisted by bowler-hatted 'Bulldogs', prowled the city after dark enforcing the law. It was also forbidden to share the company of Ladies-of-the-Night. Even that of Girls-in-the-Town was not — quite, quite . . . A Lady-to-Whom-You-Had-Not-Been-Introduced was the preferred euphemism. I was also given to understand, probably falsely, that the Bulldogs were all either ex-pugilists, or very fast runners able to catch anybody. I was also given to understand that the Proctors, though it was as well to avoid them altogether, closed an eye to the occasional visit to a pub, provided that one did not emerge from it drunk.

Being almost totally unused to drink (I still am, having become a health fiend), I quickly reached the stage of inebriation. Robert Talbot, imbibing twice as much, remained entirely in control of himself. And, indeed, of me also, whose arm he was obliged to clutch. Suddenly he whispered, 'The Proctor!' He pulled me into a dark place. A bowler-hatted silhouette approached. 'The Proctor would like to see you, sir.' We emerged. The Proctor, gowned, doffed his mortar-board. 'Your name and college, sir.' Too befuddled to be much surprised at being so respectfully addressed by a university don, I managed to mumble out the required information. Next day, or thereabouts, I appeared before the Proctors. I was fined — I'm not sure, now, but let us say — two pounds, whereas Robert Talbot, drinking twice as fast, was fined only one. He was considered to be engaged more in looking after me than in transgressing. I felt embittered. I also suspected favouritism, the Proctor hailing from Talbot's college. Absurdly, of course. The Proctors were not so much concerned with what amount of the sacred liquid resided within my stomach, which was little; as with what degree of possession I exercised over my person, which was less.

Amongst the lore, true or false, poured into my receptive ears, was the story of the undergraduate given to delving into the ancient University Statutes. Many of these, it was said, had fallen into disuse but had never been rescinded. This young man, wise beyond his years, when hauled up in the street, after giving his name and that of his college, demanded that the Proctor should read to him the lesson for the day. The Proctor produced from his pocket a New Testament, and did so. But if undergraduates can acquaint themselves with old and discarded university statutes, so can Proctors. Next morning the miscreant was fined not only for his original misdemeanour, but had a further fine imposed on him for appearing before the Proctors improperly dressed.

He should have been wearing long yellow stockings, cross-gartered.

During my first year at Oxford, my vacations were spent with Uncle Tom and Aunt Ethel. They had moved down the Dublin mountains to a much smaller house and grounds where they did a little farming, and Uncle Tom also worked as Secretary to the Protestant Orphan Society at their Dublin office in Molesworth Street. Additionally he edited the Dublin diocesan magazine, *Our Church Review*, in which he published one of my early articles. I often bicycled over to Uncle Lennox and Aunt Dolly at Sorrento Cottage in Dalkey. My elder sister Eileen was with our parents in India, and my younger sister Maureen also, until she was due to begin her medical studies at Dublin University.

The late Dermod O'Brien, portrait and landscape painter and President of the Royal Hibernian Academy, proposed to take a large party of guests, perhaps twenty, to a Christmas-time fancy dress ball at the Gresham Hotel in O'Connell Street, Dublin. He had Algerian costumes made in his house for everyone. I was over from Oxford for my Michaelmas vacations and was invited. In preparation for this, Uncle Lennox took me to dancing lessons in Dublin: foxtrot, quick-step, modern slow waltz, old-time quick waltz, tango. With his usual sardonic tight-lipped smile, his eyebrows drawn up and forehead crinkled in amusement under his boyish shock of hair, he trailed his long thin form through the dance steps under the instruction of the lady teacher. There was not time for many lessons.

We assembled in the large foyer of the Gresham Hotel, all score of us, sitting on chairs or on the floor to form a group. The orchestra sounded from the adjacent ballroom, and the dancers flitted past the doorway. Dermod O'Brien, benign, paternal, a great party man, paired us off. I, not yet twenty, immensely green, with only one term at Oxford behind me and therefore almost straight from the monastery of a boarding public school in the isolation of the Dublin hills, found myself having to cope with an experienced girl of perhaps twenty-three.

The orchestra paused. It would start again in a moment. What would the voice of the band leader announce? My ears stretched themselves; my heart fluttered. A foxtrot or a quick-step I could manage best. A lot of it was like walking, and I had more or less learnt how to turn and how to get round the corners. Failing that, oh please let it be a fast waltz! Somehow or other I would be able to twirl around. A slow waltz I feared; it needed precision and control. A tango, on which we had spent the least time it not being much danced, would be out-and-out terror.

But what is this that the voice is announcing? A Paul what? I turned to my partner for elucidation. 'It's a Paul Jones,' she said. A Paul Jones! What horror was this? Why had that fool teacher not taught me how to dance a Paul Jones? She had never even mentioned the existence of such a thing! In panic I watched the couples in our party one by one rise and depart. A single resolve filled my head; I would not budge from my position on the floor until the next dance came along. We were the only two left. My partner was looking more and more restive. 'Let's dance,' she said. I stumbled, a walking corpse, to my fate.

We entered the room. Everybody was dacing a foxtrot! How could a Paul Jones be a foxtrot? Everything I had learnt about *chasses* and turnings left my head. I just walked the Experienced Girl backwards before me up the room, round the corners, and down the other side of the room. How I prayed that the poor thing would somehow be able to escape from me! The orchestra stopped in the middle of a bar, then broke into a gallop. The Experienced Girl smiled, thanked me, and left.

A man seized my right hand. Another man seized my left hand. I was being dragged clockwise round the room, part of a ring of men facing inwards towards the girls. A ring of girls, facing outwards towards us, were turning anti-clockwise. The band stopped. The girl standing opposite me apparently expected me to dance with her. So a Paul Jones was merely a way of changing partners, of getting to know people! As I left the ballroom, the Experienced Girl was passing through the doorway with her partner. She glanced at me, said something to the man with a smile, and he looked in my direction. Any embarrassment that I might have felt was swallowed up in thankfulness that she was free.

I sat down again on my part of the floor. I found myself beside a girl only a little younger than the Experienced Girl. Her Dutch accent seemed to me romantic. The Dutch girl asked me what age I was. I couldn't bring myself to confess to nineteen, so said, 'Twenty.' It wasn't too big a lie; I was due to be twenty in a month or two. She wasn't keen to dance either, so I escaped the follies of the foxtrot and the terrors of the tango. We just leaned against one another and talked, and she became my official girl-friend for almost a year.

She was an artist. She made a pencil portrait of me which she propped up behind her on a chair, placed a mirror before her to reflect the drawing, etched the reversed image on to a flat stone, and from the stone printed off copies. So, when she later invited me up to her room to see her etchings, it was in fact to see myself.

She was fascinated by Christmas trees. When on one occasion I visited her flat where she lived with her mother and two brothers, it was to find her lying on the couch staring at the Christmas tree. She had been there two hours. Her elder brother would allow no one to tell him dirty jokes and, when he shook hands, condescendingly extended two fingers only. He said that it made people respect him. I have often wondered since how long it was before somebody hit him on the jaw. A frequent visitor to the flat was the Dutch consul. Although he had been in Dublin for ten years, he still spoke English with a thick Dutch accent.

I have never before nor since met a household so devoted to food. Mother and daughter talked food during its lengthy preparation. As the family made its way through the gigantic meal spread on the table (I always had to give up at the half-way point) they analysed the food. As they cleared the table afterwards, they held a post mortem on the food. During term time at Oxford the Dutch girl encouraged me to write love letters to her. She described them as beautiful and poetic. They were certainly immensely long. One day she startled me by pulling open a large drawer. It was packed from edge to edge with my letters, each letter tied up with a purple ribbon. I do hope that they have been burned long since, used perhaps to light the range prior to preparing the food. I'm ready to lay a bet with any man that they were an unconscionable load of rubbish.

It was in my first term at Worcester College that I won my only cup. Because of my short-sightedness I had to abandon rugby football, and I took up rowing. At Kinsale and nearby Sandy Cove in County Cork I had learned to row tirelessly mile after mile. But river racing in 'shells' bears about as much resemblence, whether in finesse or the exhausting demands it makes on the body, to tugging along a sea boat, as racehorses running the Derby bear to a carthorse drawing a load of coal. Still, I had learned to pull an oar and to feather it, so they appointed me stroke to one of the two fours which were to race for the Worcester College Freshman's Cup. The boats used for preliminary training, though light by sea-going standards, were rudely known as 'tubs'. They were clinker-built, and had neither outriggers nor sliding seats. My tub won.

A few days later my 'scout' (college servant) came to tell me that, as stroke of the winning crew, I was due to take over a cup from the previous holder. The latter begged me to collect it as soon as possible. When I saw him he said that it was somewhat large, very much in his way, he kept it under his bed, and occasionally used it for a purpose which the donor perhaps had not envisagd. Somewhat large! It was enormous, and gave me the impression, falsely no doubt, that it was made of tin. I too kept it under my bed.

By the Trinity term I was already showing the first modest signs of becoming a health fiend, at least to the extent of taking up sunbathing. Come summer, and Parson's Pleasure was sure to be crowded with male undergraduates, and even rather strangely shaped older dons in deckchairs, taking the sun completely in the nude. The privacy of this patch of grass, situated on one bank of a branch of the river Cherwell, was secured by high palings. There was even a paling projecting half way across the narrow stream to mask the sunbathers from the view of ladies passing in punts up and down a neighbouring reach. A fatal arrangement . . .

On rare occasions an innocent, not knowing what lay beyond the river half-barrier, would pole his punt, cargoed with mothers, aunts, sisters or girl-friends, round the partition and plunge them into a world of male nudity. Many of the denizens of Parson's Pleasure would take a pleasure far from parsonic in watching the victim (it is no easy manoeuvre to turn round a long vessel with a single pole) struggling to extricate himself. I myself always identify with the victim, whether it be an unsuccessful stage comedian or whatever, and would watch in acute anxiety. I mentally divided the victims into upper middle-class punts and lower middle-class punts. (I suppose it's just possible that aristocrats and labourers might go in punts.) From lower middle-class punts would come, after an initial hush, suppressed giggles. With upper middle-class punts the silence was more profound and painful, barely punctuated with strained low-voiced little attempts at conversation.

Why couldn't the half-river barrier have borne a warning sign: NAKED MEN, or, more genteelly, it being I suppose a university structure: UNCLOTHED MALE PERSONS? Failing that, why couldn't the paling have been turned to a practical use, frankly advertising itself as a peep-show for women, with properly designed viewing points in the shape of keyholes? To give it dignity, above could have appeared the University coat-of-arms, with Gothic lettering (dark blue, of course) reading: WHAT THE HOUSEMAID SAW. A toll could have been levied and the proceeds devoted to the maintenance of the fabric of the colleges. A belly dance by, say, a Regius Professor of Divinity, alone should have netted a sufficient sum to endow a new Chair.

Robert Talbot carried out, from time to time, well conceived pub crawls with a friend at Keble whom I shall call the Divinity Student. (Why are divines, in their early years, often such rascals? There was St Paul. And John Donne.) The Divinity Student owned a powerful Norton motorbike. Robert Talbot on the carrier, they would set forth with the intent of lowering two gallons of beer each. When Oxford met Cambridge in a motor cycle rally, the Divinity Student was pressed, sometimes even after such an evening, into riding for Oxford the following day. As part of his studies, he learnt classical Greek. This he wrote fluently and badly. There were few Oxford public houses the walls of whose urinals did not bear Greek inscriptions which, being translated, conveyed such messages as, 'God (Zeus), I needed that pee!' Fuelled as he was with two gallons of beer, he was able to reach incredible heights. These were duly recorded on the wall with a neatly ruled pencil line and a figure stating the altitude as measured from floor level.

None could approach this extraordinary man in this field of human endeavour. He was, compared to the ordinary chap, what a high powered fire-fighting hose is to a watering-can. Blues and half blues are awarded at Oxford for high jumping, long jumping, running, throwing weights, a dozen things. But for his event, alas — nothing. Indeed, I feel it to be so taboo that I fear to mention his name. And so this great Oxford athlete, later doubtless a luminary of the Church of England, must remain for ever unsung. It is a deep pity, for it can truly be said of him that no man ever aimed higher.

Chapter Four
Girls In Oxford

In my second year at Oxford I wanted to break away from the pattern of vacations spent with Uncle Tom and Aunt Ethel. I was conscious that I was involved in the painful but necessary business of leaving the nest — painful, because it involved some hurt to two wonderful foster-parents. It was towards France, and towards increasing my small stock of French, that I spread my wings. In the Michaelmas vacations I made my way to Val André in Brittany. Why Val André? Because it was a small place and I feared, having so little French, to encounter a large place like Paris; and because it was the only place in France where I had stayed for any length of time. On my second return from India, after our tour of Italy, my parents and I had spent a summer fortnight there. The beach had been crowded. In the garden sunshine I had daily lessons in French from the village schoolmaster. But now, at Christmas time, with a bitter wind blowing off the Atlantic, not only had I to force myself out once a day for a brief walk through deserted streets, not only were the hotels and *pensions* almost empty (I was the sole resident guest in a forty-bedroom hotel), but many of the proprietors had departed to Paris for Christmas.

My English tutor at Oxford was the aforesaid Dean of Worcester College, the now late Colonel Wilkinson. His large sitting-room, where I went to read my essays to him, seemed mainly to consist of shelves of books rising to the ceiling. If a book that he wanted wasn't there, he disappeared into a mysterious bedroom. I *assume* that there was a space for a bed in it, but almost as many books emerged as came off the shelves of the sitting-room. When reading to him my essay on Dryden, I announced that the date of a poem, *The Medal*

I think it was, was such and such. Colonel Wilkinson corrected me by a year or two. But I had been to Delphi and consulted the Oracle. 'Professor Saintsbury,' I countered, 'said so.' George Saintsbury's history of English literature was my standby, as I imagine it was that of half the School of English. Colonel Wilkinson disappeared into the bedroom. He emerged with a first edition (his entire library seemed to consist of first editions) of *The Medal*. He brandished the title page at me, with the date on it. He was right — as usual. 'Professor Saintsbury sometimes makes mistakes. Oh,' he added quickly, 'he's a great scholar. He's a very great scholar.'

I don't want to give the impression from the foregoing that I was an ardent student of English literature. On the contrary, I was determined to be a writer and had no particular interest in getting a degree. It had come as something of a shock to find to what an extent the course was slanted towards producing critics and teachers; how it involved one in reading other people's books rather than in making one's own. While still at school I had vaguely supposed that I should at Oxford be taught the construction of novels and plays. Later I discovered that certain American and Canadian universities did so teach.

Colonel Wilkinson set me an essay on Samuel Butler's *Hudibras*. Once again I am forced to be cautious, because of the long lapse of time, and to say that I think it was *Hudibras*. No where, for some reason or other, could I find a later publishing of this; it seemed, if I was to do my essay, that I must get hold of a first edition. (I know now that a collected edition of Samuel Butler's work appeared in the eighteenth century, and another at the beginning of this.) I went, as ever, to Basil Blackwell's second- hand book department where all the old, and therefore usually most expensive, books were to be found.

I had heard from a fellow undergraduate that Colonel Wilkinson had been able to pick up cheaply many a valuable book from second-hand shops whose owners didn't always know what treasures lay upon their shelves. He had bought a first edition of Samuel Butler's *Hudibras*, so the undergraduate averred, for half a crown in a Glasgow bookshop. The undergraduate made it clear, however, that *Hudibras* (if that was the book) was not a particularly valuable first edition; worth two guineas, perhaps. So I walked into Basil Blackwell's with hope.

Unfortunately the only copy they had was a special presentation copy given to King James II. It was bound in calf leather and the edges of its pages were heavily coated in gilt. Hungrily I gazed at this beautiful book. It would be the crown in my modest collection. But it was five guineas, a large sum in those days, and a huge sum in the scale of my income and taking into account how much I already owed Basil Blackwell's. I bought it. For three rapturous days I alternately gazed at it and got on with my essay. But on the fourth day, with my essay concluded but not done really well, I decided that my debts were too pressing and that I must sell it back. I told Basil Blackwell's my story and they gave me four guineas.

Somehow the word got to Basil Blackwell himself. At least I assumed at the time, from the authority with which he dealt with the matter, that the gentleman who descended the stairs was Basil Blackwell, and I have so thought ever since. 'If I had known of your difficulty,' he said, 'I should have lent you my own copy. I'm just driving home. Won't you come with me?' We went to Boar's Hill, as I remember.

Later I sat down at my table in my top-storey room at Worcester College to improve my essay. Before me lay the as yet unopened first edition. My mother had a maid in Ireland, a dashing girl, who always used to say when she broke a piece of china, which was frequently, 'It came apart in me hands.' I opened the cover of the first edition and — it came apart in me hands. The string or cord with which so many old books are bound had hardened with age, lost its flexibility, and become brittle. Imagine having to go back to a man who has lent you a first edition (oh, not a very valuable one, but nevertheless a first edition) and having to say to him, 'Thank you very much for lending me your first edition. Very useful it proved. Oh, by the way, the first thing I did was to rip the cover off.' In the goodness of his heart all that he said was, 'Don't worry! I can easily get it repaired. I only wish that it had come apart in *my* hands.'

Colonel Wilkinson advised me to acquire a special knowledge in one facet of English literature. He suggested the plays of Beaumont and Fletcher. So all the works of Beaumont and Fletcher I duly bought, in ten large volumes, and took them with me to Brittany. Every day I sat in the empty lounge of the hotel at Val André and waded through these plays, hardly able to tell one from the other, with great gusts of boredom sweeping over my mind. Somebody said that, for Beaumont and Fletcher, lust consisted in lust for a number of women, whereas love consisted in lust for one woman only. And indeed whoever said that wasn't far out. I tried telling myself that my Uncle Lennox's comedies didn't read nearly so well on the page as they acted in the theatre; that a play was only half alive until it had a stage performance. But it didn't succeed in stifling my yawns. Recently my ear caught the names of Beaumont and Fletcher on my radio, to which I had been only half attending. The speaker added, 'Two very dull authors.' So I am not alone!

To Colonel Wilkinson, his tall form with the upright carriage of a soldier standing at the lectern of Worcester College chapel, his strikingly handsome and powerful profile and bald crown bent over the Bible, his beautiful bass voice reading the lessons beautifully (I was told that in later years he became largely inaudible), I shall always be grateful for the pleasure he gave me Sunday by Sunday. Against those lectures of his in the College hall on Andrew Marvell and Butler, that passed largely over my head and left my notebook empty, I hold no grudge. But for Beaumont and Fletcher I shall never forgive him. I wouldn't wish it upon my worst enemy that he should make himself an expert in Beaumont and Fletcher. I believe that all persons convicted of a felony, before being committed to jail, should be given the option of reading Beaumont and Fletcher, all ten volumes of them, from beginning to end, and then successfully sitting an examination in them. Or it might simply be used in place of the death penalty.

I said that the hotel lounge in which I worked was empty but for myself. This is not quite true. There was a single visitor, an elderly gentleman, who sat in it for half hour every morning while he sipped two whiskies, and for one hour every evening while he sipped three. In all the weeks that I was there, his routine never varied. I longed to speak to him, but couldn't find the courage to break, with my small store of French, a silence that he seemed determined to maintain. This small store was growing no larger since I hardly spoke to anyone; there was almost nobody to speak to. Then, somehow,

I increasingly got the impression that he wasn't French and that he spoke English.

I conveyed to the proprietor that my stay was coming to an end and that I must shortly settle my bill. When my parents had asked for the bill in restaurants, I had heard them use the word 'addition'. So, 'addition' was what I asked for. 'Je veux mon addition, monsieur, s'il vous plaît.' He put his head on one side. 'Bien, monsieur, mais . . . La livre, elle monte' — he raised his upturned palms towards the ceiling — 'elle descend' — he reversed his palms and lowered them towards the floor. The pound had just come off the gold standard and was indeed mounting and descending, generally the latter, on the foreign exchanges. But, he added, he would see his banker next day when the bank was open. In the winter, it opened only once a week for half a day.

It was the banker however who called the next evening at the hotel. He held a preliminary conference with the proprietor in an adjoining room. Meanwhile I sat at my usual table with my ten volumes of Beaumont and Fletcher about me, while the elderly gentleman was ensconced by the fire in his usual impenetrable silence sipping his third whisky. The proprietor and the banker entered. I pushed aside Beaumont and Fletcher to make room for them. But instead of using the word 'addition', the proprietor used the word 'note'. 'Monsieur,' he said, looking alternately at Beaumont and Fletcher and at me, 'quant à votre note . . .' 'Note'! What was 'note'? The banker joined in and started using it also. The greater my expression of bewilderment grew, the more frequently and loudly they used it. They might as well have been saying, 'Paul Jones'. Now was the time, if ever, that I needed Beaumont and Fletcher to inspire me. But the volumes lay there dumbly like slabs of suet.

I looked appealingly across at Old Whisky. His face remained impassive. I now felt certain that he was English-speaking; that, in fact, he was English. He didn't look French. That he spoke French I knew, at least sufficiently well to order whisky fluently. 'Bon soir, Monsieur le Patron. Trois Scotch, je vous prie.' He always ordered the three together, and marshalled the little glasses before him. On leaving, he always said, 'A demain' — till tomorrow — 'monsieur!' I didn't know enough French then to detect whether he spoke with an English accent.

When things reached a total impasse, at last he broke down. 'He wants you to pay your bill with a cheque made out in francs.' Ah! In that way, no matter how the pound was faring at the moment that the cheque was presented at my Oxford bank, Monsieur le Patron would get his due amount of French money. I wrote the cheque. The proprietor and the banker departed. I beamed at Old Whisky. 'I thought you were English!' 'I'm American,' he said. I laughed lightly, as at a piece of hair-splitting. He drew himself up. 'It's not the same thing, you know.' How wrong he was! At that moment it *was* the same thing. What mattered such trifles as the American War of Independence or the breadth of the Atlantic ocean? Through our common language he had been communication, he had been enlightenment, he had been help — he had been everything that mattered. In a blinding moment he had pin-pointed the fact that 'la note' meant 'the bill'. He had succeeded where Beaumont and Fletcher had failed.

In my Hilary vacations I went to Paris. No more empty streets, no more empty buildings, no more days of silence, no more bitter wind off the Atlantic — just Paris in the spring! It was to an alleged French family in the boulevard Saint-Michel that I made my way. The 'family' consisted of a widow who put up students, half of whom were French, and the other half British, Canadians and Americans. I advertised in *Le Figaro*, in the extraordinary shorthand used by French newspapers (jeune étudient de l'université d'Oxford, became j. étud. de l'univ. d'Oxford), for persons willing to exchange their French against my English. I got sixty replies. (Everybody, I was assured, wanted to learn English.) It was perhaps as well that I did. Despite all the drilling I had received at school that the French did not say, 'I am thirsty', 'I am hungry'; but 'I have thirst', 'I have hunger' (j'ai faim), on the first evening I entered the dining-room and announced from the doorway in dramatic tones, 'Je suis femme' (I am a woman). Hardly were the words out when I realised my blunder. I took my seat, overwhelmed by blushes and surrounding laughter.

One of these replies was from a flagellator. It said that he would not take up any of our time in my teaching him English, which he already spoke fluently, having spent his time in Africa among British people. So all of it would be devoted to his teaching me French. He made only one stipulation. His colonial career, he said, had taught him the value of discipline. I should have to agree to his whipping me if I failed to work sufficiently hard or sufficiently well. I replied to him, describing in some detail what he could do with his whip. He answered commending my 'sense of humour', and asked me to take tea with him. I wrote to him no more.

One other matter of college discipline needs a mention. It was obligatory to be in college before midnight. The gates were then locked. To enter after that time involved 'climbing in'. Only a few of the more daring spirits attempted this. In the case of Worcester, the illegal entry was effected at the far end of the very extensive grounds where there was a junction of river and canal. How it was done, was once described to me. I found the description too involved to follow, probably because I lacked interest. I had not the slightest intention of risking being 'sent down'. Yet I once found myself out after midnight, though in unusual circumstances. My solution, however, was nothing like as spectacular as that of Brian Fitzgerald (as I shall call him). Brian Fitzgerald had been with me at my Dublin preparatory school. There we, the sons of the Protestant Anglo-Irish Ascendancy, were educated to be more British than the British themselves. When Brian Fitzgerald undertook anything, it was always spectacular and always ineffective. Becoming irate, he would shout abuse at the object of his ire. At the same time he would shake his fists above his head, his arms fully extended. He thus rendered himself incapable either of striking his adversary or defending himself. Although a few of us went to Irish public schools, the majority at that time found their way to English establishments. Thus I lost contact with Brian Fitzgerald — until he turned up at New College.

Lennox Robinson had written the script for a film, *The Blarney Stone*, being made by Tom Walls at Elstree. My uncle wanted me to join him there for a day and a night. I obtained the necessary twenty-four hour permission to be outside the two mile (was it?) radius of a circle with its centre at Carfax. So I had, of course, no need to be in Worcester before midnight. But I didn't go to London. Instead, I was inveigled by a girlfriend to spend the day with her in Oxford. (Some years later we met again by chance when I was writing in Chelsea, and she became my wife — now, alas, my late wife.) When I had seen her back to her father's house in Walton Street, it was just after midnight. Thus the position, as it appeared to me, was that while I had every right to be outside Worcester provided that I was in London, I had no right to be, since I was in Oxford. It was a balmy summer night. I therefore resolved the dilemma by simply lying down on the grass by the river and falling asleep. About five in the morning a voice said, 'Hello, hello! What have we here?' I opened my eyes, to see a pair of boots. The boots were surmounted by a long pair of dark blue trousers. I ran my eye up the trousers, and found a policeman at the top of them. I explained the situation. He made a note of my name and college, and I heard no more about the matter.

But of course it was very different for Brian Fitzgerald. He invited me to a party at his rooms in New College. He had done some solo flying, but wanted to carry things further by joining the R A F. He had a minor heart murmur which showed up when he was unfit, but not when he was in training. The party was a last fling before getting himself into shape. I left fairly early. But next day I learnt that he had issued out with the last of his guests to see them back to their colleges. As he returned, the midnight hour struck. To gain entrance, at some point he had to scale a high wall. But there was no one to give him a leg up. He made good the deficiency by wrenching out the headstone of a grave. When caught (Brian Fitzgerald was always caught), he was thus brought before the authorities not only on a count of illegal entry, but also on one of desecration. How the matter ended, I never learnt. The last I heard of him was when he was arrested while crossing O'Connell Bridge in the middle of Dublin. Wearing a blue shirt, he was shouting slogans, carrying a suitcase in his left hand, and waving a revolver over his head with his right. (Once again, over his head!) In Italy, Mussolini had formed his Blackshirts. In Germany, Hitler soon copied him with his Brownshirts. In Ireland, Blueshirts followed. Their purpose was to protect the meetings of the party on the right in favour of Dominion status, against the attacks of Republicans on the left. Predictably, when Brian Fitzgerald was searched, the revolver was found to be empty, and its ammunition in the suitcase.

What of Colonel Wilkinson and women? My greatest interest in Oxford was — girls. (They still remain a major concern.) Yet I never fell foul of him on this score. With the same sweeping simplifications of youth, it was held by those in my hearing that all women

53

undergraduates were plain, and that it was to the town that one must look for glamour. And, of course, to those Swedish girls who came to Oxford to learn English. Those blonde Swedes! Heaven lay in their blue eyes! Superficially, the above judgement was true. Daily, on their bicycles and their way to lectures at The Schools, there would sweep down St Giles, from Lady Margaret Hall, Somerville, St Hugh's, St Hilda's and St Anne's, a great swarm of crows in their unbecoming black gowns and caps, and dark stockings (were they blue?). But of course, under those black feathers, were sparrows and starlings and parakeets and nightingales and birds of paradise. Certainly my eyes, despite the excellence of the lecturers, spent much of the time at those same Schools roving over those same crows.

My first actual meeting with them, however, was an unhappy one. It was my second or third term, spring was in the air, and I was invited, along with seven other men whom I didn't know, to — was it Lady Margaret Hall? Why me? Had I been vetted by the KGB, MI5 and the Proctors? Anyway we were taken down to a lawn off which four punts floated, ready to receive us. A lady with a commanding smile arranged us into four crews. Male and female created she them; a man and a girl in the bow seat, a man and a girl in the stern. As I was in a stern seat, I volunteered to pole us along. Though I had never poled a punt in my life, I was a seasoned rower of sea boats and anticipated no difficulties.

Fortunately we were the sternmost of the four punts. As I zigzagged my way along the Cherwell, first almost colliding with the left bank, then with the right, sometimes nearly dragged off the stern decking on which I stood as my pole stuck in the mud or entangled itself in the weeds, we fell further and further astern. I noticed that the conversation of the other three had dropped into a murmur. There was a giggle. Then I overheard a girl's voice saying, 'No, it's not fair!' The man in the bow announced that he would take over the poling. By a tremendous effort, he caught us up with the rest. I then offered to relieve him. Fatigue and frustration had cost him his manners. 'Oh no, you don't!' We landed. A picnic had been arranged for us on the bank. I melted away and walked back to Worcester. Soon afterwards I had made myself into an expert, disengaging from the cling of the river with a sharp twist of my wrists or just allowing the weeds to slip away, and keeping the pole close against the side of the hull.

Chapter Five
C'est La Vie!

In the Oxford Trinity vacations I travelled to the south of France as an *au pair* to a French family. They enticed me with assurances that they were midway between Nice and Cannes, and that I could visit either resort whenever I chose. They omitted to mention that, although they were indeed midway between, or rather equi-distant from, Nice and Cannes, it was at the apex of a triangle that extended backwards from the coast and upwards some two hours' car drive into the foothills of the Alps; and that, the only time that I ventured to ask for a day off in Cannes, they would indeed grant the request, but with a total lack of all graciousness.

They stated that they would meet me at the station in Nice. I replied that there was no need for them to trouble to do this; that I could perfectly well take a taxi. But they wrote again reiterating very firmly that they would meet me with their car. When I reached Nice I at once, giving up my ticket, made my way to the front of the station. Not finding them there, I returned to the arrival platform. It was a slack moment between trains and there were few railway officials about. I finally decided to go to the front again. Just as I was doing so a train arrived, people flooded about me giving up their tickets, and the collector asked me for mine. Despite my conversational exchanges in Paris I was still very short of French, but managed to convey the outline of the situation to him. He refused to accept my word. He summoned a policeman who mounted guard over me.

When, years later, my wife Margaret and I were staying in Normandy at Dieppe, with visits to Rouen, I suddenly realised one day that the Normans weren't behaving according to my ideas of

French people. Where were the gesticulations? Where was the vivacity? Where were the dark complexions? Where was the smaller stature? Why, they were tallish, and phlegmatic, and didn't wave their arms about, and had brown hair! They — they looked British! Of course, 1066, the Battle of Hastings, the Norman Conquest! (I was always mustard at History.) They *were* British, and the British were them, at least partly! And as one went south to Paris the people were darker, less tall, and more vivacious; and when one went further south still, to the Midi, to the Côte d'Azur, they were like those Italians that I had over-topped in Rome in my schoolboy cap! So I stood within sight of the street passers-by feeling foolish as I stared down at the top of the helmet of the miniature policeman, though no doubt he would have proved very efficient had I tried to escape.

My host, a *commandant* in the French army, appeared, accompanied by his American wife. She spoke French as well as English, whereas he spoke no English but understood it fairly well. I explained my predicament, there followed a voluble argument between the policeman and the commandant, the latter pulled his army rank for all that it was worth, and I was released. I travelled in the back seat of the car with the nine- year-old son. I discovered that I was not to teach him English, but the whole range of school subjects through the medium of French. Well, all the better for my French!

As we left the Côte d'Azur further and further behind and penetrated further and further into the Alpes Maritimes, I at last attempted to pierce the daunting half-hour silence that had brooded over the front seat. 'No wonder,' I said laughing, 'that you didn't want me to take a taxi!' I was an innocent yet; there was still another hour and a half to drive. The silence from the front seat deepened, as did the dusk of evening. On arrival, husband, wife and son bundled out of the car without a word and disappeared into the house. I was still recovering from my astonishment, and apprehension as to what I had let myself in for, when an English girl appeared with a lantern. She too, I learnt later, was 'au pair', and was there as a nurse to the nine-year-old son, the five-year-old daughter, and the three- year-old baby of the family, also a son. The spinster sisters who did the cooking and the cleaning, a French couple from Nice, were au pair likewise. The relatively large household was founded on shifting au pair sands.

Perhaps the house itself was built upon, if not sand, at least something almost as unstable. It was brand new and constructed of concrete which, as the house settled into its site, had developed fissures in the walls of the bedrooms. Great and frequent were the lamentations thereat, and many the curses in French and English that were heaped upon the head of the absent builder. Even the garden was new. In fact, most of it had not yet emerged above the ground. The house was called 'Les Peupliers'. But where were the poplars? I discovered them at last lining each side of the concrete drive, their average height about six inches. Well, Rome wasn't built in a day (though the house itself looked uncommonly like as if it had been).

At the table, French fashion, the meat was served first, and the vegetables followed. The English girl and I insisted on having them together. The Commandant was always served before anyone else. The veins standing out on his forehead, he wolfed down the meat, eating himself into a daily indigestion. The sweet, always a small suet pudding or a flan of some sort, in other words a round structure, was with mathematical precision segmented by Madame the American so as exactly to fit the number of the company, plus one segment over. This last furnished a second helping for the Commandant. No one else was ever offered one. The English Girl and I left the table famished. We took turns to slip away to the village to buy great blocks of a dark raw local chocolate.

Madame the Americn had been brought up by her mother in Belgium where she had learnt French and Flemish, then she was married to an Austrian and had learnt German and Hungarian, they had taken their holidays in Italy where she had learnt Italian, and after his death she had married mon Commandant. She discovered that we were bringing chocolate and biscuits into the house. Furious at this slur upon her hospitality, she began to rate us. As it was our own money that we were spending, and neither of us had the smallest intention of starving at her behest, we simply stared at her with all the independence of au-pairs who weren't being paid a sou, and she relapsed into frustration.

The concrete bedrooms opened in a row off the concrete passage. Monsieur and Madame were at the far end of the passage. Then came the children in two rooms. The bathroom followed. The ladies from Nice were boarded out somewhere. The English Girl and I occupied adjoining rooms in the remainder of the passage. Each of our rooms had a key. There was a communicating door between our bedrooms, locked, and with no key. My natural powers of inspiration had now undergone a two-year development under the scholarly disciplines of a great and ancient university. One day, with a flash of genius possible only to an Oxonian, I asked myself the question: is it possible, just possible, that the key of my door also opens that communicating door? Swiftly academic theory was translated into that practical experimentation that is the only true science. I inserted the key. The door opened.

The English girl was reclining on her bed in a négligé. In a few disciplined strides I was upon her, kissing her. She lay still, accepting my kisses. Then, unaccountably, my genius deserted me. They say down Wimbledon way that, in lawn tennis, one should never change a winning game. In a moment of folly I did just that. In a word, I ceased to kiss her and began to tickle her. With a shocking suddenness she broke into wild giggles, sufficiently loud not only to awaken the Dead, but even possibly Monsieur and Madame. Not all my pleas could still her. At this grave juncture my academic training reasserted itself. Realizing that an immediate retreat from the room was, strategically, the only sound policy, I carried out a planned withdrawal as only an Oxford man can — in blind panic. Next morning she laughingly asked me how I knew that the key fitted. With the simplicity of greatness I answered, 'Just a hunch!' Thereafter I noticed that the key had vanished.

Madame made a number of attempts to get me to speak in French at the table. If everybody present had been able to speak only French, or only English, I should have spoken French without inhibitions, or at least not too many of them. But somehow the mere fact that Madame and the English Girl spoke both languages fluently tied me up in a tongueless inferiority. The English Girl's ladylike English contrasted oddly with her gutter French. Educated in a huge impersonal Paris state school, while her mother spent most of her time and money in gay fashionableness on the Riviera, the English Girl's French expressions frequently caused Monsieur and Madame to raise their hands in horror or amusement.

After I had been there a month, Madame made a fresh attempt to get me to speak in French. 'My son tells me that you speak to him all the time in French. My husband doesn't speak English.' Monsieur stepped in to save me. 'Ça m'est égal. Je peux comprendre assez bien l'anglais.' So I continued to confine my French to my pupil for a further week or two, after which I found the courage to speak it at the table also.

It wasn't easy to concentrate on the task of teaching him. At nine years of age he masturbated not consciously, not in any easily recognizable fashion, not now and again, but almost continuously. His right palm placed on the seat of his chair, his legs crossed about his wrist and over his hand, he would by some means or other work himself up into an ever heightening tension, reach a climax and break into a sweat, there would be a brief period of relaxation, and then the whole process would start up again.

There was no justice between child and child. He was the child of the first marriage. The five-year-old daughter and the three-year-old son were the children of the present marriage. The three-year-old, the baby of the family, was the darling around whom the household revolved. If he took a toy from his sister, and she merely tried to get it back again, it was she who was punished. She was even on rare occasions tied down in her cot by her wrists to the top corners and her ankles to the bottom. It was averred by Monsieur and Madame that insect bites that would be innocuous in a temperate climate could be dangerous in the summer sub-tropical heat of the Midi. The nights were loud with the sounds of the crickets and a million insects and reminded me of India. So when the baby was bitten, the household was turned upside down while he was given, on the doctor's orders, half-hourly warm baths to draw the poison in his body into an abscess which could then be excised. In the event he neither died nor produced an abscess, but merely quickly recovered. As for my pupil, he was largely ignored.

What good then, I reflected, to draw his attention to what he was doing, let alone try to prevent it, in this household in which injustice and lack of affection reigned unblushing and supreme. Doubtless it was but the expression of, and release to, many insecurities within. At a later time I asked an Oxford friend, who had taken over from me after I returned to Oxford for my next term, how he had dealt with the matter. He replied that he had come to the same conclusion as I, and had done nothing. When I also asked him, somewhat jealously, what he had thought of the English Girl, he answered after a judicious and prolonged reflection, such as one would expect from a Keble College man, 'She had breasts that stuck out nicely.' With this judgment I found myself able to concur.

There were a few vegetable features in the garden that rose to some height. There was the tree in front of the house. Under this I sat in a deckchair to read *When Lovely Woman . . .*, my Uncle Lennox's latest play of which he had sent me the typescript. On returning it, I wrote comparing it with Farquhar, Goldsmith, Sheridan, one or two others. I meant to be flattering. Actually, I had no decided reactions to it whatever. He replied wishing that I had seen less in it of Goldsmith and more of my uncle. Only twenty-one, I was a far from mature critic, especially in the matter of visualizing how a script would act out on the stage.

One day cries arose from under the tree. We rushed out, only to see Monsieur le Commandant lying flat on his back. The deckchair had collapsed under him, trapping his fingers as he tried to save himself. The weight of his own sturdy medium-height form was crushing his hand and he was totally unable to move. He stared up at us as we bent over him. The sweat of pain had broken out on his brow, but he allowed no further sound to pass his lips. His wife often spoke with pride of how, in the First World War, he had as a volunteer gone up in flimsy fighter planes often almost 'tied together with string', had been shot down — and had gone up again. Between us, we raised him. His fingers had suffered no lasting damage, but we heard him groaning upstairs as the circulation returned to them.

He was devoted to his wife. One day as he sat at the head of the table and she stood by him with her arm about his shoulders, he tapped proudly with the back of his hand on her pregnant belly. But his eye could stray. Deep in my university books a day or two later, I heard her voice shrieking out in French from an upper window. It emerged, as I listened, that he had taken the English Girl with him to the garden's other main above-ground feature, a fig grove some distance away. He was vehemently assuring his wife that the object had been solely to assist him in the collection of figs. But Madame continued to allege that he might well have tasted of some other fruit. However, the hurricane of words at length abated.

Not so long after, as the English Girl sat on the dining-room cum sitting-room couch, he knelt down before her to assist in removing her shoes, the straps of which were causing difficulty. I thought nothing of it. But the two spinster sisters from Nice had apparently seen deeper and further from the door of the kitchen. After the Commandant and the English Girl had departed, but while I was still in the room, the ladies from Nice returned to the door. Their eyes were saucers. 'Did you see the way,' exclaimed the elder, 'that he was looking up her legs? Did you just see the way he was looking up her legs?' 'Yes,' chimed in the younger, 'did you see the way he was looking up her legs?' They continued for the space of some two minutes to marvel at the way he had been looking up her legs. At this point the elder seemed to feel it to be the moment to wind up the subject and draw a conclusion. 'C'est,' she said, throwing up her palms to heaven, 'la vie!' Her younger sister nodded sagely. 'Oui,' she agreed, 'c'est la vie!' They vanished. The rattle of crockery arose.

I had arrived into the heat of the Midi in the then conventional clothes of Oxford, a jacket and flannels. Monsieur and Madame both urged me to adopt cooler wear, preferably beach pyjamas. Next day I came down to 'petit dejeuner' at least without my jacket and tie, my shirt collar open, and my sleeves rolled up. My host and hostess expressed a qualified satisfaction.

On my day down in Cannes I bought myself two pairs of beach pyjamas, the first in dark blue wool, the second in a flaring red canvas. I was surprised that wool should be used in a hot climate. But, with the sun blazing down on my head and beating up from the pavement into my eyes, I found the wool in fact to be pleasantly cool. It was much more comfortable than the canvas. I should not now be surprised. Dry heat is comfortable, but wet heat is insupportable. The canvas, being impervious, kept in the sweat and created more. The wool, being porous, let in the air and let out the moisture, and also absorbed it off the skin.

Wearing the blue short-sleeved T-shirt that went with the wool trousers, I was self-conscious about my thin unmuscled arms. On giving up rowing after a year, I fell physically into poor shape. Then one day my Oxford friend from school days, Robert Talbot, produced the slim volume of Lieutenant Muller's 'My System', perhaps the most widely sold system of 'free' exercises, that is exercises without the use of apparatus, ever published. Robert Talbot allowed the exercises to lapse after a couple of weeks, but I borrowed his book and did not. I still do them in an adapted form. Then he bought an expander, but used it for only about a week. However I didn't, until years later, follow him into the path of apparatus. As I passed a shop window in Cannes, I glanced at it apprehensively to see how my dreaded arms appeared. Behold, a miracle! They were rounded and muscular. And I had been doing the exercises for only a few months! As rapidly as I had lost the physique that rugby football and rowing had given me, I had regained it again.

With renewed confidence I presented myself, on my return, in my blue wool beach pyjamas. Monsieur and Madame beamed upon me, the Commandant even exclaiming, 'Monsieur Dorman a une jolie taille.' The English Girl went so far as to stretch out her leg under the garden table at which we were having supper and caress my calf with her instep.

But if the blue wool had proved successful both socially and as an aphrodisiac, the red canvas certainly did not; at least not on the political plane and with Monsieur le Commandant. He had two great hates, Communists and Italians. 'Les sales Italiens!' The adjective 'sale', dirty, was never omitted. 'Ces sales Italiens' — these dirty Italians. It was only a few years before Mussolini was to deliver his stab in the back to a France reeling before Hitler's onslaught, by marching his troops in over the nearby frontier. Monsieur's face was a study in hostility as I walked into the room in my red canvas trousers, widely flared out at their bottoms 'à la Mexique', as the label in the shop window had declared. 'Communiste!' He looked really violent, as though he no longer saw the person inside the red canvas but only the Communist party advancing upon him. Later that day an army friend paid a visit. Monsieur introduced me to him as 'l'instructeur de mon fils'. He added some reference to the red I was wearing and to Communists. The army visitor nipped in tactfully. 'Communiste en couleur, mais pas en sentiment!'

Monsieur and Madame would sit on the couch, while Madame read to him, translating into French as she went, sleazy American magazines. On one occasion, after a particularly lurid passage, she looked at me with round serious eyes. 'We read these magazines,' she said, 'just to see the kind of thing that goes on.'

They were for ever discussing in shocked tones the state of undress in which the women in Cannes and Nice went about. 'Mon Dieu, presque nues!' It was an almost daily topic at meal times. To my twenty-one-year-old physical-culture eyes the majority of these women had seemed tanned indeed, but flabby and unhealthy. I could not feel that, in summer, the close sweaty heat of a huge city like Nice (I accompanied the family down to it several times when they went shopping) was conducive to health, except perhaps along the sea front. The Alpes Maritimes, yes. Endless sun, the freshness of the endlessly blowing 'mistral', wonderful! When they asked me my opinion as to the state of undress of the women, I replied that it hardly mattered, since they were so lacking in attraction. At once Madame and Monsieur leapt to their defence in, respectively, English and French. 'Oh no, there are some extremely beautiful women; mais non, ce sont des femmes fort belles!'

Monsieur kept hens. Every evening, when getting them into their cages, he would increasingly lose his temper as the silly creatures ran this way and that. He used a branch that he had broken off from the tree to lash at them as he abused them violently. Perhaps he saw them as Communists or Italians. 'Ces sales poulets!' On at least two occasions he killed a hen by kicking it in the neck.

He became convinced that a dog was killing his hens at night. I felt, though I refrained from saying so, that there was really no need of a dog as he was doing very well on his own. He decided to watch for the dog. All night he sat out in the deckchair under the tree, a rug about his shoulders and armed with his two service pistols. In the early hours I heard a shot. I went to my open window and gazed out through the insect-excluding zinc gauze. I saw a great foolish peasant face, its chin apparently resting on the ground. Then I realized that the peasant was making his way up the sunken track in a farm cart, and was standing up in his seat to see what had happened. 'Were you firing at me, monsieur?' 'Non, non!' The Commandant was hastening forward, all apologies. 'Mais non, monsieur, I was not firing at you. A dog has been taking my hens. I was firing at the dog.'

The combination of almost ceaseless sunshine and bracing air produced in the inhabitants a high degree of health; or would have, but for a cheap and potent local wine. What the bountiful heavens gave, the bistro took back, at least from those who visited it frequently. Such a one was a gardener whom Monsieur and Madame employed at erratic intervals, that is, during such periods as he was not serving a prison sentence for wife beating. When he was in gaol his wife, whose complaints to the police had put him there, would devote her battered person night and day to getting him out. Flushed with success, she would bear him home. He would do a spell of gardening, sooner or later quench the resulting thirst at the bistro — then beat her up again. She would point out the fact to the police, and he would be clapped back behind bars once more. Ah well, as the sisters from Nice would almost certainly have said, 'C'est la vie!'

Back at Oxford (I was there for four years) I felt, despite my dancing lessons with Uncle Lennox and a great deal of practice since, the need for more. Girls, girls, girls; they filled a large part of my head. No doubt a large part of the heads of the girls concerned were filled with boys, boys, boys. It was the pre-mating season, the time of selection. Robert Talbot suggested that we should go to such and such an address where the two daughters of a clergyman ('each more beautiful than the other,' he assured me) gave such lessons. Without troubling to work out this philosophical conundrum, I clutched at paradise. And later, indeed, at one of the daughters, who told me to watch where I put my hands. Well, I *was* only a learner. However, she ended up by being very nice to me, and we met again. And not in church either.

At St Columba's College I had shown myself to be outstanding at English, in my first term gaining a prize as the best writer of prose in the school; and later becoming the editor of the school magazine and winner of an essay competition open to the public schools of Great Britain and Ireland. As a consequence, the Warden wrote to my parents in India advising tht I should be sent to Oxford, which he said had the best School of English. But was all this really a qualification for an Oxford English course? Not really. The courses then on offer were either one heavy on linguistics, Old Icelandic, Old Norse, Old English, whatever, and lighter on Literature; or one lighter on linguistics but heavier on Literature. I chose the latter as, for me, the lesser of two evils. What I needed was a third choice, one lighter on the course of English literature from Anglo-Saxon to recent times, and heavier on the analysis of journalistic markets and the preparation of articles for them, the construction and realisation of novels and plays, the production of verse in all the rhyme schemes and in none, and in all the meters and in none.

The instinct to make books, as compared with the instinct to study them, can be very different, despite there being a connection. (Indeed, there can be a marriage.) Oxford's answer, at that time, would have been that there were other places where this could be done. But was this a valid answer? Again, not really. There were universities on the North American continent that offered courses in creative writing. No postal course could have the impact of a college tutor, the companionship of services in a beautiful chapel and meals in a beautiful hall, the university buildings (as one approaches by rail, there across fields and rising above trees are the 'dreaming spires' still intact), tea and muffins dripping with butter with a girlfriend in one's rooms on a summer afternoon, eight purposeful oars in unison on the Isis or one languid pole on the Cherwell; above all, the prestige, the prestige, the prestige of Oxford. It still has power to cast a purple glow about me.

Chapter Six
Women In Chelsea

When I came down from Oxford I joined my parents and sisters at our house, 'Lackaroo' at Crosshaven in County Cork. There I passed the time in bathing, tennis and the pursuit of girls. These important activities I had to suspend at the end of the summer when 'Lackaroo' was let and my parents returned to India, bearing my sisters with them. I went to my Uncle Tom and Aunt Ethel. I involved myself, at my father's wish, in the hopeless hope of securing a literary position in a publisher's or some such by answering, from the depths of the County Dublin countryside, advertisements in London newspapers and periodicals. Opportunities for such employment in Ireland were then few, and not much more numerous in England.

Uncle Lennox saw my predicament and swept me away to London. He settled me in the Euston area, into the Oxford and Cambridge Mansions, where resided his great friend Norris Davidson, an Irish Cambridge graduate engaged in filming documentaries. My father furnished a small allowance of three pounds a week. Though of course worth much more then than now, it didn't enable me to afford the Oxford and Cambridge Mansions. In any case one name alone burned in my brain — Chelsea. Chelsea was Bohemia. Chelsea was romance. Every writer must go to Chelsea.

Uncle Lennox had hardly departed from Euston station, when I departed too. I found myself in the Kings Road by the Town Hall. On the other side of the street was clear evidence that I had not been mistaken. There was the former Chelsea Palace, across its facade in burning letters, 'Ca, c'est Paris'. Romance indeed — Continental romance! I could hardly wait to get inside. The show turned to be pure British music-hall at its far from best. The only Continental connection was when a Frenchwoman, with most of her teeth missing, came on to the stage to gum out the title song in a muffled voice.

My unfurnished room, at fifteen shillings (75p) a week, was at number nine in Oakley Street. I furnished it with a book-case that I formed simply by nailing together planks that I had sawn into lengths, and by a cheap inflatable air-bed or mattress spread on the planks of the floor. The book-case, which was tall and narrow, reared up to within a foot of the ceiling and was filled with my Oxford books. The air-bed at once developed a leak. But I was determined to get value for my money out of it. For some weeks I pumped it up at every bedtime, although I knew that, come an hour later, I'd be resting on the floor for the remainder of the night. Eventually I bought a divan.

I also acquired two fifty-six-pound dumb-bells, a large mirror, and a commode. The mirror was to assist in the correct performance of my dumb-bell, expander, and free exercises, and the commode went with it, being in the same lot at the weekly auction of the Army and Navy Stores. I tried to leave the commode behind, but — no. No commode, no mirror. The rule of the auction was that, at your own expense and forthwith, you had to clear away everything in your lot. So all that I could do was to make a joke of the commode, open the lid, and offer it as a seat to my guests.

One of the most successful parties I gave consisted of a group of men and girls, non-religious all, sitting in a circle on the floor, myself presiding over them from the commode, drinking tea, and reading out passages from the Bible for their beauty as prose until four in the morning. Where parties are concerned, there is no accounting for what will go and what will flop. A successful party is a group spontaneity; it comes unbidden, and flees if the attempt is made to repeat it.

Our regular night life consisted either of coffee and conversation at the candle-lit Blue Cockatoo on the Chelsea Embankment; or of tea and conversation, with table-tennis and dancing to records, at the Chelsea Studio Club close to the Town Hall. Few of us had the money ever to order any food at the Blue Cockatoo, but they tolerated our sitting there for hours over a cup of coffee because it drew in a well-to-do clientele who came to gaze at us, fancying that they were beholding Bohemia. Years later I came across a book of reminiscences in which occurred the passage: 'The candle-lit Blue Cockatoo, where beautiful girls gazed into the eyes of villainous-looking young men with beards.' So that was us! It wasn't a period for beards, and if you had one it tended to mark you out as being either a painter or an art connoisseur.

The majority of those who haunted the Chelsea Studio Club were aspiring painters, with three or four writers and a couple (almost the only two earning any real money) of architects. There was an inverted snobbery which made it *de riguour* to be poor; having money was something to which one did not readily admit. One of the architects, excusing himself, said to me, 'The thing about architecture is that it's only half an art, and half a business. People have got to have houses. It's ridiculous, but just for designing a clock, which I can do in ten minutes, I get a guinea.' Well, half an art or not, for me it's among the greatest of the arts. I have no precise knowledge of it, but I have an insatiable appetite for finely designed buildings of all periods, and their settings.

As for the table-tennis and the dancing to records, I had an enormous enthusiasm for both. My two chief dancing partners were the Lustful Married Woman and the Lesbian. The husband of the Lustful Married Woman was never to be seen. All that one ever learnt about him was that he had a hairy chest. As the Lustful Married Woman and I gyrated with the minimum of movement to the gramophone with its '78' ten-inch records, we clung to one another. She had a soft not particularly well-shaped body and a pretty face. Whether dancing, or standing beside me while I rewound the gramophone, she talked incessantly of sex and men. It wasn't that she was aiming to be either sexy or a bore. It was just that it never occurred to her that there *were* any other topics.

It was the era of the brief reign of the Italian boxer Carnera as world heavyweight champion. His publicity billed him as 'The Man Mountain', his dimensions being given as six foot ten and twenty stone. But on a later occasion I saw these figures reduced to, respectively, six foot seven and eighteen stone. I was sitting at a table in the Chelsea Studio Club with the Lustful Married Woman and a serious young man whom I had noticed around but had not met before. We were drinking tea and discussing Carnera's size. The

Lustful Married Woman, with a gleam in her eye, remarked, 'He must have huge genital organs.' 'Oh no,' said the Serious Young Man earnestly, 'not necessarily. It's probably only about two inches long.' After reflection he added, 'Just imagine twenty stone driving that!' The Lustful Married Woman sat sipping her tea and imagining it, her eyes gently rolling.

At a dance being given at a friend's house, and apropos of nothing in particular, she suddenly said with a gay laugh,' All the men seem to come to these parties on a permanent erection, and something's got to be done about it.' Later in the evening, when we were sitting out watching the dancers, she clutched my arm in a painful clasp, as might a naturalist when catching an unexpected glimpse of the Loch Ness monster, and hissed in my ear, 'That man over there's having an orgasm.'

If dancing with the Lustful Married Woman was sex, dancing with the Lesbian was art. No longer the minimum of movement. Now all was energy and complicated steps, chassés, double chassés, outside chassés, outside double chassés, an assortment of twirls. You name it, we embroidered on it. The Lesbian was, on the physical plane, savagely anti-male. She had a vixenish, but also witty, tongue. Yet she took a liking to me from the moment that I joined the club, and I enjoyed her wit, her magnificent piano playing, and her good dancing.

At one party in the club I heard her snarling at a man who, in the crowded room, had quite inadvertently brushed against her while trying to reach the service hatch. I heard another man saying to him, 'She's an awful creature! She's just done the same to me!' Once she said with a grin to a girl who commented on how much we danced together, 'He restrains himself.'

Poor lass, she had no idea how unprepossessing she was. Her mouth was filled with the blackened stumps of teeth. She couldn't eat properly and seemed to live on cups of coffee. Once, at a dance at an artist's studio, while continuing to hold my hand she drew out our two arms to their full length saying, 'Look at the difference between them!' Mine (I was wearing a short-sleeved T- shirt), much developed by my fifty-six-pound dumb-bells, must have been five or six times as thick as hers, which were little larger than just the size of the bone.

She was fiercely independent and kept her address a secret. We learnt however that it was a small basement room which she had at a reduced rent in exchange for filling and stoking the stove of the central heating system of the building. We didn't like to think of her, in her emaciated condition, heaving buckets of coal. But she had a constant feverish coffee-stoked energy.

My principal girl-friend of the moment was an attractive American poetess from New York's Greenwich Village. We bickered ceaselessly. Once, when we were boarding a bus at Knightsbridge, I exclaimed in exasperation, 'You make me feel sick!' — and then became aware of grins on the faces of those around us. On a walk, whenever I admired anything in a passing London view, she at once compared it unfavourably with what New York had to offer. My mother used to say, 'Comparisons are odious.' How right she was!

As I tapped out on my portable typewriter (I now had a table) short stories which were invariably rejected, the American Poetess reclined on the divan and scribbled out poems. The only line of hers that I can remember was, 'And Sabra urinated on the roof.' Sabra seemed to appear in most of her poems, generally urinating, and always in the strangest places: in cellars, behind dust-bins, in gutters.

The American Poetess was at all times ready to take off her clothes at the drop of a hat, or perhaps one should say at the drop of a pair of knickers. In a friend's room she proposed so to dance, and the Lesbian said that she would accompany her. Before disrobing, the Lesbian approached me and said earnestly, 'I haven't got any breasts, you know, and I've never menstruated.' I replied that neither had I, and that I should be very pleased to watch her dance even under those circumstances. Like a Roman emperor I reclined beside the girl owner of the room on a divan, and the dance commenced. During it the Lesbian made what are technically known as 'passes' at the American Poetess. But the latter was entirely male-orientated, was really dancing for me, and took avoiding action. As they ended the dance and approached the divan, the Lesbian said with a rueful grin, though without any trace of rancour, 'She wouldn't lecher with me.'

At length I could stand no longer the bickering with the American Poetess and we parted. One piece of literary encouragement I did owe to her. On occasion I wouldn't work for the whole of a day, not out of laziness but frustration. My father had, by implication, given me two years in which to establish some sort of a literary career, that is, until his retirement from India. My frustration derived not merely from my failure to get any of my stories accepted as time ran out for me, but even more from my consciousness that I was unequal to the task at that time of creating fictional characters or of infusing interest into my material. The American Poetess said to me, 'I knew an artist in Greenwich Village who felt just the same as you do. But he said that when he started to make some sales and to acquire a style of his own, then he couldn't stop working.' I treasured up this saying long after she had gone.

On my parting from her, she immediately took up with a young poet, one of our circle, in the room next to mine. And the wall between was extremely thin . . . This she did, not in any way to get back at me for having abandoned her. I may have found her a pain in the neck with her automatic 'odious comparisons', but hers was a generous nature. It was simply that, for her, life without a man was unthinkable, even for a moment.

The lady who ran the Chelsea Studio Club also owned two or three nearby houses and rented out mostly single rooms to her members. Thus, quietly and unobtrusively, standing behind her service counter in one corner of the club room, serving simple snacks to those of us who had a few coppers to spare, or watching us dancing or debating or playing table tennis or exhibiting pictures, she encompassed our lives. Thinking back, I feel that she ran her small enchanting domain with very little in the way of thanks. La belle dame sans 'merci', as Keats might say. Except that the belle dame was, in fact, rather a plain Jane. Save on one occasion. It was a very rare fancy dress party. She appeared behind her counter in an exceedingly low-cut dress, displaying most of a magnificent pair of breasts. The Lesbian, who seldom saw life other than in extremes, informed me, a total invention of course, that all the men were running wild and sinking their teeth into them!

The family returned from India. After settling into 'Lackaroo' at Crosshaven in County Cork, my father and mother travelled over to England on a brief visit. I met them at the station and we bused to Chelsea. I had sold nothing. As I pushed open the front door, a large envelope lay on the mat. I opened it at once. Before our very eyes was a cheque for half a guinea, accompanied by a copy of *The Writer* dated June 1935. The competition had been for the best epitaphs to an author and to a free-lance journalist respectively, in four very short lines of verse and according to a pattern that we had been given. I had been unable to think up a good epitaph to a free-lance, but fortunately no one else had been able to either. For good measure I had composed two (with J. B. Priestley and Charles Dickens in mind) for an author. There, in the magazine, were printed the names of the sixty-nine competitors left after the first elimina- tions, and there among them was mine. Twenty-nine names remained after the second scrutiny, and there still was mine. The third sifting left but nine names, mine among them. The final adjudication was between three of us. 'The prize is awarded to Mr. Sean Dorman . . . Here are his two epitaphs to an author:

> Garret bare,
> Forced enslavement.
> Hempen noose,
> Angel Pavement.
>
> Budding Dickens
> Thought it 'swell';
> Ed's regrets,
> Little Knell.'

The words danced before my eyes in silver and gold. My three pounds weekly allowance had not been utterly in vain. It was extended for a while longer.

Apart from the two architects, the only other member of the Chelsea Studio Club making much money was a girl photographer. She had a big studio, was tall and lanky, wore white trousers and a white broad-brimmed hat, and had large teeth which stuck out in a considerable disarray. One evening, during a party which she was giving, she asked me to pose for her on the following day in the nude. I replied that I would do no such thing. She then said that I might wear a towel. 'Round my middle?' I enquired. 'No,' she said, 'round your neck.' While dancing with her, she asked me if I would enjoy being given a bite. I replied that that was a joy that I was prepared to deny myself. The next moment I was conscious of a piercing pain in the lobe of my ear. Angrily pushing her away, I left her. I know that it is my function as a writer to be able to understand all sorts of natures. But, at the time, I found it impossible to understand why any man should be turned on, by having his ear almost scythed off by an angular female with teeth like a rapacious yak.

If the American Poetess had given me a general encouragement with my writing, the Lesbian did it in more specific terms. 'You should try writing articles, Sean,' she said. 'They're much easier to do than stories. I sold an article about a walking tour that I did on the Continent. I was never there at all. I just got all the stuff out of guide books. Later I found that I had made myself cross a bridge that had fallen down the year before.' This last item could well have been apocryphal; she was given to embroidery.

I knew that either Sandown or Ventnor on the south coast of the Isle of Wight were apt to head the British sunshine and ultra-violet irradiation tables. Indeed, with nostalgic memories of Cannes, I had been down to Sandown as a second best. I looked up an ordnance survey map. What with the sandy beaches of Sandown, Shanklin and Ventnor, and other stretches of sand just under the sea, I caused myself, wearing only bathing trunks and carrying a rucksack, to have made a hike along nearly the entire south coast of the island, when necessary travelling at low tide. Graphically I described how, in the heavy going on the sand, I was able to average only two miles an hour. I sent it to a health magazine, it was instantly accepted, and back came a cheque for a guinea.

Nothing could hold me now. I concentrated on articles on sunbathing and sunlamps (carbon-arc and mercury-vapour). During 1936, 1937 and 1938 there followed in a brilliant succession into the pages of such magazines as *Health & Strength*, *Health & Efficiency*, *New Health* and *Vigorous Health* articles with such titles as: 'Restock Yourself With Sunshine', 'Sun-tan — Not Sunburn', 'The Sun — Friend or Enemy?', 'To Acquire That Tan Hasten Slowly', 'Help Yourself to Sunshine', 'Bringing the Sun Indoors', 'Let Dr. Sun Give You a Tonic', 'Sunbathing in the Home'. I was for the most part paid a guinea a thousand words, about the lowest rate of payment made at that period. *New Health* paid two guineas. The

Thames was on fire. A new voice was being heard in the land. Picasso had his blue period. I, with a more penetrating vision, pushed my way beyond the visible into the invisible during what the world has come to know as my Ultra- Violet Period.

In 1938 this merged into my possibly even greater period of creativity. There must be few living who need to be told that I refer of course to my Infra-Red Period. I suppose that the most celebrated of these treatises was that which appeared in an issue of *New Health* under the title, 'How Infra-Red Cures Disease'. That I got most of my information out of the brochures of the manufacturers of infra-red lamps is neither here nor there. Other magazines that I wrote for were *Health For All*, *Superman*, *The Bicycle*, *Armchair Science* and *Sunbathing Review*.

When 'The Cambridge Review' attacked nudity on the Cam under the title, 'The etiquette of the River', I immediately saw how, by putting this together with my memories of Parson's Pleasure at Oxford, I could earn another guinea. This I did in a torrent of sententious clichés in my article, *Nudity at Oxford and Cambridge*. 'Is he not aware,' I cried, 'that the human organism hungers and thirsts for direct contact with sunlight and air, as a doe for the springs? How does he suppose we shall banish ugliness and ill-health from our midst, save by a return to the elemental sap of nature? Will he not exercise just sufficient patience, or at least avert his fastidious regard for just long enough, to allow us to reattain something of the stature of the Giants that were before the Flood?' Ugh!

I escaped out of 'health' into other topics, and into other periodicals such as *The Lady*, *The Cork Examiner*, *The Writer*, and Uncle Tom's Church of Ireland diocesan magazine, *Our Church Review*. I was also engaged in 'ghosting' half a dozen books for a London publisher. When the 'author' of two of these books died, my mother, in a spirit of irony, sent me the following cutting (expurgated by myself) from *The Irish Times*: 'Yet "—"'s claim to rank with Martin Cobbett, "The Druid" and Arthur Binstead rests upon the merits of his books; his story of "—" ' (ghosted to my certain knowledge by someone else) 'is probably the most popular; *his study*' (the underlining and the exclamation mark were in the handwriting of my mother) 'of "The—" *the most brilliant!*' (ghosted by myself). 'Who cannot vividly recapture the speed, rhythm and stamina of — winning the Derby in—'s *wonderful account of the race?* It is safe to predict that each of the books *that seemed to glide from his pen*' (this time the underlining is mine; I can't resist it!) 'will become classics in the literature of the Turf.'

I spoke of two books of his that I had ghosted. I never so much as saw him after our initial introduction. In the case of the first book, and urged on by the publisher, I did my best to contact him, but he was never there. Doubtless such an encounter would have embarrassed him. The first book was, however, at least one quarter his. Half my time went on collecting material, and the other half on writing it up. Of the collected material, the more important part came from his articles in a newspaper.

The text of, and the research for, the second book was mine, and I have letters from the publisher that make this clear. The supposed author didn't even think of the idea. That was proposed to the publisher by the illustrator. Before the book could be put on to the market, the Second World War broke out. The book was placed in cold storage. When it emerged, a final chapter was added by someone else to bring it up to date. Without this final chapter and the illustrations, the book is wholly mine. These were the glorious days before the Trade Descriptions Act! But in any case the practice of literary ghosting had since been put on to a somewhat more fair and honest footing.

In Dublin I wrote a three-act play on Van Gogh, entitled *Sunflowers in Arles*. When I sent it for criticism to Uncle Lennox, both he and his artist wife Dolly expressed their surprise at how much I knew about Vincent van Gogh. I was pleased. But I was also conscious that the knowledge I had was merely that of anyone who had studied the letters of Vincent to his brother Theo, the various biographies of Vincent, reproductions of his pictures in book form, and biographies of Gauguin, his companion in Arles. Uncle Lennox also said that my dialogue was too 'thick', that is, the speeches averaged too long. I agreed, and rewrote.

When *Sunflowers in Arles* was rejected by the Hilton Edwards-Micheal MacLiammoir Dublin Gate Theatre Company, Hilton Edwards pointed to the bookshelves in his office where were several versions by other dramatists of the Vincent van Gogh story. He proposed that I write him instead a play on the Irish Labour leader

James Connolly. I had no enthusiasm for this. But neither had I for my own play, not even enough to offer it elsewhere. I even raided two of the three copies for sheets of paper. I always use the backs of my old typed quarto sheets for further writing. When my wife Margaret in recent times, at our home Raffeen Cottage at Fowey in Cornwall, told the novelist and our good friend the late Leo Walmsley that I did this, he began doing it too! But of course I kept one copy intact; one does not lightly destroy two years' work.

About six months after the play's rejection, I was taken as a guest to the Arts Club in Dublin. The dramatist Denis Johnston called to me that his wife wanted to talk to me about my play. She started to speak, but almost at once got up and came towards me saying, 'The poor man can't shout to me across the room.' I didn't think much about it at the time, though I could have heard her perfectly well from where she was. Later, I understood the significence of her move.

She sat down beside me and said that she read scripts for Hilton Edwards and Micheal MacLiammoir. She had forwarded my play with a strong recommendation that it should be accepted, pencilling on the copy, 'Micheal MacLiammoir's part'. She said that she had forgotten that Micheal MacLiammoir wouldn't take on a part where he couldn't appear to physical advantage. (Vincent Van Gogh was an ugly man.) But, she continued, why didn't I send it to Laurence Olivier? He would take on any part that he considered worth while, regardless of the looks of the character.

I had interviewed Laurence Olivier fairly recently for my monthly magazine *Commentary*, when he was over in Dublin making the film of Shakespeare's *Henry V*. On getting home, I looked out my third intact copy. My 'intact' copy wasn't intact at all! Somehow I had wandered into all three copies. I couldn't even form one complete or near-complete copy out of the three remains. As to Betty Chancellor's coming over to sit beside me, I learnt later, in connection with something else, that she was deaf and acted by lip-reading. I could hardly believe it. I had seen her in leading role after leading role in the Dublin Gate and Gaiety Theatres, and never a sign of it.

On one occasion I was sitting close to the Gate Theatre stage; too close, as the actor's make-up could be seen. Betty Chancellor and Micheal MacLiammoir were playing a love scene from MacLiammoir's dramatisation of Charlotte Bronte's *Jane Eyre*. They were right in the corner of the stage beside me. The scene ended. I was aroused by the voice of a man behind me saying to his companion, 'There's powerful acting for you!' Powerful indeed! So powerful that I wasn't aware that it was, or indeed that anyone had been acting at all. All I knew was that I had been transported, and now abruptly found myself back in the Gate Theatre again. I had seen Micheal MacLiammoir playing Shaw's *Man of Destiny* at the Gaiety Theatre. I said to an actor friend that I had found MacLiammoir poor in the part. 'Oh,' he said, 'Micheal can be marvellous or bloody awful.' Well, I never saw Micheal Macliammoir bloody awful. But he certainly could be marvellous. And Betty Chancellor too.

Chapter Seven
Suicide Among The Artists

On the twenty-fourth of February, 1941, there appeared a small news item in *The Irish Press* which reported a meeting at the Hammam Restaurant in O'Connell Street, Dublin, of the Council for the Defence of Irish Intellectual Freedom. This Council, announced *The Irish Press*, sought the repeal of the Censorship of Publications Act. Elected officers were as follows: President, Madame Gonne MacBride; Vice-Presidents, Lennox Robinson and Mrs. Sheehy Skeffington, M.A.; Committee, Mr. Sean Dorman — and some other names.

Each time that we met I felt my position to be a little more absurd. The leading officers were no more than figureheads who never put in an appearance. Indeed, apart of course from my Uncle Lennox, I had never even met them. I can't remember which of us drummed them up. Perhaps I got hold of Uncle Lennox's name, and somebody else secured the other two. Since my second return from India to Ireland as a fourteen-year-old, I had heard the name of Maud Gonne MacBride from time to time. I vaguely supposed that she was an Irish rebel leader of some sort, but was never interested enough to enquire. One day in Sorrento Cottage I overheard Uncle Lennox saying to someone that W. B. Yeats had been in love with her, but that he, Lennox, thought that Mrs. Yeats had made him the better wife.

So there we sat in the Hammam Restaurant, a little group of eight or twelve young unknowns with no political power, making speeches to one another about the repeal of an act that had the support of the all-powerful Catholic Church in Ireland. There is nothing ridiculous in being unknown. There is nothing ridiculous in being but few in numbers. There is nothing ridiculous in trying to secure the repeal of an act that carried censorship, at least as it was applied, to an absurd extreme in the hopeless hope of cutting off Ireland from much of Western European thought. (The distinguished author Sean O'Faolain, in a fairly recent letter to me, said that it was the advent of television — British television, I presume, picked up along the east coast of Ireland — that had driven the final nail into the coffin of the obscurantists.)

But I felt in a false position because speeches were not my vehicle; the pen was my natural mode of communication. Nor was political agitation my calling. Rather was I a detached observer and recorder of the human comedy. Nevertheless later, from the larger platform of my not yet born magazine *Commentary*, I took more than one swipe at the Irish censorship as it then was.

The appearance and behaviour of our Secretary, our most prolific speaker, also made me feel like a member of an ineffective little debating society peacocking under a grandiloquent title: The Council for the Defence of Irish Intellectual Freedom. The Secretary was a tiny man suffering from some eye condition that made it necessary for him to have one large round black lense in his large round spectacles. He was always holding forth on the subject of aspects (he pronounced it, ahspects) of sex (he pronounced it, sax). 'I propose this evening,' said the round black pane of glass regarding us menacingly, 'to deal with certain ahspects of sax.' We wilted. 'Sax,' said the black pane balefully, 'has many ahspects.' We fiddled nervously with our paper bags of sandwiches brought for the interval. Eventually we came to refer to him as Ahspects of Sax. The Council for the Defence of Irish Intellectual Freedom! Against the serried ranks of jovial self-confident clerics strolling over the lawns of Maynooth College, secure in the backing of an adoring Catholic population, we should scarcely have been able to defend our sandwiches.

My wife Margaret and I escaped out of the Council into a larger and more promising venture, our Picture Hire Club. She became the Secretary, mainly dealing with the artists and collaborating with them in the hanging of their pictures. I was the porter, on occasion collecting pictures from studios and clients and carrying them through the streets. In an age when beards were more or less confined to painters, and rare enough for impertinent boys to shout out 'beaver!' before taking to their heels, I had unwillingly grown one on much pressing from Margaret. What with this and the pictures under my arm, I found myself to my resentment frequently being taken for a painter. It wasn't that I didn't honour painting and painters. I champion all the arts and all artists. It was simply that in fact I was a writer, was proud of being a writer, and wished to be taken for a writer.

One small boy's thoughts, however, turned in a different direction. It was in the second half of December, 1941. I was walking along Lower Baggott Street with a couple of pictures under my arm. As he passed me, I heard him murmur to himself, with no intention of pertness but merely as a grave involuntary breaking out of his innermost thoughts, 'Father Christmas!' That finished me. The beard came off.

Long before that, back in March, the Picture Hire Club had its opening by Dermod O'Brien, President of the Royal Hibernian Academy, before several hundred people. The Club occupied two galleries above Trueman's art shop in Molesworth Street, not far from the College of Art where the Royal Hibernian Academy held its exhibitions. This time there was much publicity in the whole of the Dublin press.

Our President was Dermod O'Brien, and our Vice-Presidents were Hilton Edwards, of Hilton Edwards and Micheal MacLiammoir Gate Theatre Productions; Lady Glenavy, R. H. A. (Royal Hibernian Academician), mother of the well known journalist and B. B. C. personality Patrick Campbell; and (yes, you've guessed it!) Uncle Lennox and Maud Gonne MacBride. Though intended once again to give us a reflected respectability and importance, and to look well at the head of our stationery, this time these 'names' amounted to rather more than that and some of their bearers gave us practical help.

The idea for our Picture Hire Club was suggested to us by an artist friend whom I shall call John Stewart. We met him while we were staying in our cottage in Donegal, later described by me in my book *Brigid and the Mountain*. To visit us, he would tramp across mountain and bog in his hobnailed boots, the only footwear that would stand up to the flinty tracks. Sitting before the incandescent ring of the turf (peat) fire, eating slices cut from a huge round maize loaf baked for us by Oona in an iron pan over her fire, with butter straight from the farm and honey in the comb, we had some of the best conversation that I have ever had.

Margaret and I tramped in our turn and in our hobnailed boots to visit him, his wife, and their baby in a large house built by an architect relative of his. John Stewart was for ever urging us (Paul, Edwina and Madeleine had not yet been born) to have children. 'They will make you feel stronger,' he said. 'Actually, you are weaker, but they will make you *feel* stronger.' He was quite right. In the evening we were startled to hear the baby, standing up in its play-pen, relieving itself in a resounding cascade on to the carpet. John was a great reader of Freud. It was he who first pressed Freud's *Totem and Taboo* into my hands. Convinced that house-training would inflict a trauma on his offspring's mind, he permitted it to let fly at the carpet at more or less regular intervals and with a complete abandon. Perhaps the carpet eventually suffered a trauma.

John Stewart was a tremendous reader of other books also. While we were there he was making his way through Tolstoy's *Resurrection*. He became so engrossed that on one occasion he read it for twenty-four hours very nearly non-stop. His wife told us that he looked quite wild-eyed in the morning after one of these all-night reading sessions.

He averred, perfectly seriously, that people didn't want pictures. What they wanted on their walls was a dart-board. He himself desired to be a writer. Writers, he said, had more power. He was much offended when I told him that he couldn't possibly be one; that he wasn't capable of composing even a postcard. This was the literal fact. I never saw from his pen anything longer than a postcard, and it was full of unfinished sentences. I don't mean that he had a telegraphic leaving-out-verbs style ('Wednesday fine. All well here.'). I don't mean that he ended in a row of dots, leaving it to the reader to complete the inference in his own mind ('There will be chocolate cake with a fresh cream filling . . .'). I mean that he would write something like, 'Looking forward to seeing Margaret and you on We are all well here. Bring with you Yours, John.'

While his wife and child were away visiting her parents, he had us over to keep him company and to sit for our portraits. I'm glad

81

now that Margaret made me grow a beard at that time because, since I have regrown one since, the portrait now looks like me. As we sat before him starving and far from warm, he would never offer us any food. It was simply that he forgot. He would drag himself away from his easel, hasten to the pantry, rush back with a loaf and, as he continued to paint with his right hand, dig with his left into the bread and transfer morsels into his mouth.

Famished, we later peered into the pantry to help ourselves. The stench was considerable and we retreated. On the departure of his wife and child, he had neither cancelled nor cut down on the bread, milk and meat deliveries, and there they were, stale, sour, or bad, accumulating on the shelves. Without waiting to have her portrait done, Margaret decided that it was time for us to return to our maize loaves and our turf fire, which in the north-west highlands was necessary even in the summer.

He planned, when we all returned to Dublin at the end of the summer, to give an exhibition of his work. One day he called in at our cottage with a handbill that he had had printed in Letterkenny. In line with his conviction that people didn't want art, he intended to entice them by keeping his prices very low and having his leaflet looking as near as possible like a list of groceries. It was set up in poor type on paper of a repulsive pink.

Prices for pictures at that time would be something like five, ten, fifteen, twenty, twenty-five guineas; perhaps forty, fifty, sixty, seventy-five guineas for someone better known. For an outstanding artist like Jack B. Yeats, the brother of W. B. Yeats the poet, the price would be more like a hundred and fifty guineas. Victor Waddington, Dublin's most important art dealer at that time, once remarked to me that seldom a week passed without his selling a Jack B. Yeats for a hundred and fifty guineas. But whatever the standing of the artist, or the size or difficulty of the work, the price would almost always be stated in round figures and not below five guineas, what with the costs of mounting, framing, glazing. But John Stewart had prices printed like 1 gn. ('guinea' not even written out in full!), 1½ gns., 2 gns., 2½ gns. and, in the case of a particularly large oil landscape, a dizzy 3 gns.

Margaret felt that it was perhaps time that she took him in hand. After a severe struggle she got him to agree to double his prices and get rid of the halves. When he further agreed to her arranging his exhibition in the (former) Country Shop Restaurant in St. Stephen's Green in Dublin, she eventually quadrupled his prices, had the word 'guineas' printed in full, and on good-quality paper. But she couldn't be there all the time to manage his affairs. So she worked shifts with him. During his shifts, still convinced that nobody wanted art, he did his best to dissuade people from buying his work. Word of this came to Margaret's ears. She took him aside and explained that the idea of holding an exhibition was to sell one's pictures. She succeeded in convincing him — only too well. On at least one occasion, when someone left without buying a picture, he pursued him (the Country Shop was a basement restaurant much frequented by artists) up the stairs and on to the street. After that she gave up and withdrew to run her own Picture Hire Club.

Without one ounce of malice in his make-up, he eventually lost us both our flat out in the suburb of Clontarf and our gallery in the centre of town. He achieved this by a devastating honesty that laid waste people's relationships more effectively than the intrigues of a dozen Iagos could have done. He would talk to people by the hour, including our landlady and the owner of the building in which was our Picture Hire Club. Anything that anyone said to him he would tell out again to anyone, with a total lack of distortion, malice — or tact. He told the truth, the whole truth, and nothing but the truth, and thereby created around himself a very wilderness of human havoc as he sauntered with engaging grin upon his amiable way.

He was a born painter. He couldn't stop painting (except for a talk or to get buried in a book). When our Clontarf landlady lent him a tray, unable to resist the expanse of wood that it presented, he took it out to the sea wall and covered it with a seascape done in oils. When he returned it to her with apologies, she hung it on her wall. Excited by colour, he had neglected his drawing. Finding this going against him, he humbly put himself back to art school in his thirties and laboured among teen-agers to master draughtsmanship. His work progressed so rapidly that, within the space of a year, I noticed it pass through at least four distinct styles and always towards a more personal developed one.

D. H. Lawrence thought that furniture should frequently be rearranged about the room, and pictures frequently changed, as otherwise both eventually failed to be seen by an eye cloyed with familiarity. Out of this arose the first Picture Hire, put into effect by Harrods of London. Other Picture Hires followed in England. But our gallery at 24 Molesworth Street represented, we believe, the first importation of the idea into Ireland. *The Irish Independent* reported, 'The stationery of the Picture Hire Club shows two bonnie cherubs holding a frame over an imaginary building. This building was to have been the Customs House but, when the artist sat down to draw it, the police shooed him away.' Poor John Stewart (for he was the artist) in trouble with Authority! And all because he was generously, and without charge, trying to help us! But it was wartime, and all sensitive areas, including the area of the port, had to be closely watched.

As the capital of a neutral country, Dublin hadn't instituted a 'black-out' but merely a 'dim-out'. It thus constituted an admirable signpost for the German Luftwaffe who, after flying over a blacked-out Britain, picked up its lights before turning north to bomb industrial Belfast in the 'Six Counties' and thus, of course, a part of the United Kingdom. Political differences or not, to the Eire government the people of Belfast were fellow Irishmen. The Dublin Fire Brigade dashed across the border to assist in coping with the fires.

The Dublin anti-aircraft defences, on the occasion of the next German incursion, opened fire. As the shells burst about the aircraft, the Luftwaffe pilots, in their haste to escape them by gaining height, jettisoned their bombs, causing the usual toll of injury and damage. Some fell near to the suburb of Clontarf, on the way into central Dublin. There was no basement to the house in which we lived. Never have I felt more helpless, nor so much a kinship with every creature of the field that ever burrowed or bolted its way into the bowels of the earth when danger threatened from above. But of course all this is not worthy of being mentioned in the same breath with what the United Kingdom endured.

Doubtless a protest was lodged with Berlin. At any rate, as far as the ordinary citizen could perceive, the Luftwaffe no longer used Dublin as a staging post. On a part of the stretch of seaside street leading from Clontarf into town, concrete blocks were erected on the road surface to prevent the rapid advance of German tanks towards the city centre should an invasion occur. One block would stretch from the left side of the roadway to the mid point, the next from the right side to the mid point, and so forth. John Stewart remarked with his slow grin that the only effect of this seemed to be to slow up the progress of the Number So-and-so bus.

'The organisers of Picture Hire,' continued *The Irish Independent*, 'are a young couple, Sean and Margaret Dorman. Sean comes from an old Cork family. For the annual gathering of the family, Dormans arrive by the score.' I suspect that the journalist got this final item of information out of Lennox's, Tom's and my mother's book *Three Homes*. 'Tall, with a small red moustache and equally small and red beard and dark blue eyes, he himself is the author of that delightful burlesque at Lord Longford's garden party last summer. He met his petite Wiltshire-born wife at Oxford.'

Red beard and moustache! This, though correct, startled me. I had always assumed up to that moment that they were of the same colour as my hair, which was brown. However, if the *Sunday Chronicle* was to be believed, my beard at least had changed colour by the next day. The report started with my wife, 'Dark-haired attractive Mrs Sean Dorman, wife of Lennox Robinson's nephew. English girl, whose family is closely associated with art and literature, Mrs Dorman met her husband at Oxford — he is a graduate . . . Sean, tall young man with a fine *golden* beard is a writer and playwright.'

Margaret had included me among her many men friends at Oxford, and I her among my many girl friends, but then we lost touch with one another. Some years later, through the intervention of her younger sister Pepi Gillies (then Wharton) and Pepi's first husband Michael Wharton, author, journalist, contributor to *Punch*, who were living nearly opposite to me in Oakley Street, we met again in Chelsea. We were married at the Chelsea Registry Office. Margaret's family were indeed 'closely connected with art and literature'. Pepi Gillies studied painting in Oxford at the Ashmolean under Sir William Rothenstein, and has since exhibited and sold with great success.

The headquarters of the anti-academics was provided by the White Stag Group, whose gallery was set up by Basil Rakoczi and Kenneth Hall. Basil Rakoczi, of Hungarian parentage, had already exhibited at the Goupil Salon and the Royal Society of British Artists.

He had divorced his wife who was still over in England. He described to us with some relish how his solicitor had managed to secure for him the custody and care of his son. In spite of a number of visits to, and at least one party at, Basil Rakoczi's studio, I never once set eyes on the boy, to such a degree did his father keep him to himself and out of his public life. Basil was a small man, and it never failed to strike me how Japanese he was in facial appearance. In comparison with the rest of us, he was very well off. Part of his money came from psycho-analytical sessions which he held frequently. When asked what his qualifications were, he would reply that he had himself undergone a full Freudian analysis.

His relationship with his partner in the running of the White Stag gallery, Kenneth Hall, was not only artistic but also homosexual. I betray no confidence. They made no secret of the matter, as why should they? On one occasion it had an outcome funny to others, though not to themselves. Although then unlawful, homosexuality was not to my knowledge sought out and persecuted. But one day, when Margaret and I entered the Country Shop restaurant, a strange tableau was set before us. There was Basil Rakoczi seated at one table sipping coffee, his companion not Kenneth Hall but — a girl! There at another table sipping coffee was Kenneth Hall, his companion — a girl! As far as the eye could interpret, Basil Rakoczi was not aware that Kenneth Hall was in the room. As for Kenneth Hall, Basil Rakoczi was a complete stranger to him; never seen him before. It was hard to say who looked the more awkward as they sat bolt upright on the edges of their chairs, Basil Rakoczi and Kenneth Hall, or the girls.

The explanation was drifted to us by friends. A priest, or some priests, it was alleged, had nudged the police into taking action against a coterie of foreign artists of doubtful morals, divorcees and the like (there was no divorce in Eire; only legal separations), who were polluting Holy Ireland with homosexual practices and heaven knew what else. Hence the hastily cobbled- together ménage à quatre. Basil Rakoczi, we learnt from him, had even rushed off to the police to impress upon them that he had been the innocent part in his divorce and had been awarded the custody of his son. The day passed and so did the panic. The ménage à quatre was dissolved, and the former ménage à deux restored.

Kenneth Hall was a withdrawn man of great independence, great pride, and great poverty. If I had once upon a time lived in Chelsea on three pounds a week, he, with prices steadily rising because of the Second World War, was living in Dublin in his own room on two. If he was slow to offer help to others, it was because if he gave his word he meant to see it through. When Margaret and I at a later time asked for help from our artist friends in setting up a stall to sell my magazine *Commentary* at the Dublin Book Fair in the Mansion House, while many rushed to say yes, Kenneth Hall said no. When the day came, no one was there — except Kenneth Hall. He said that he could spare us an hour. By the time that he left, he had given us four.

Only a young man, he was already threatened with a growing deafness. Then he began to find it increasingly difficult to pass food through his digestive system. He went repeatedly for medical tests. They told him that they couldn't find the cause of the blockage. Perhaps they just couldn't find the words with which to tell him. I don't know; I'm only guessing. Perhaps he guessed too. At any rate he wrote neat little notes to his friends. Then he put on his long black quilted dressing-gown, filled his room with flowers, and lit joss-sticks. It wasn't a theatrical gesture. He was an introvert. He once said to us, 'I like to keep my private life private.' It was just that his life was important to him. But he saw no hope. So he wanted to honour it by leaving it as worthily as might be. He had lived with dignity on two pounds a week, and he died with the same dignity on the same sum.

When Basil Rakoczi found him lying with his head in the gas oven, his comment was, 'It was very naughty of him.' If the comment strikes the reader as trivial and distasteful, it must be taken into account that some years later he wrote to Margaret, when reporting the suicide by drowning of his own beloved son in the Caribbean, 'Thank heavens he chose warm water, ducks!' He was a psycho-analyst teaching release in the place of tension; doubtless in his own eyes he was practising what he preached. He had a point of view, and a sort of courage.

The summer brought the usual wilting of art that overtakes capitals, when people move to the seaside, theatres close or turn to pot-boilers, concerts are not, and artists vanish to beauty spots to fill their canvases against the coming autumn. In Ireland, our artist friends mostly went to the breath-taking West, to County Mayo or to Connemara. We went west also, to our cottage in the Donegal highlands at the foot of Mount Errigal, accompanied by our friends Noel and Margot Moffett. Noel was an architect.

The son of a Cork businessman, he was in the town-planning department of the Dublin Corporation. He got his architectural degree at Liverpool University, and studied in London under the famous Russian architect Serge Chermayoff. While Margot and he had been staying the previous winter on Achill Island, he had built for Major Freyer behind Corrymore House the first open-air theatre in Ireland. During his Donegal visit he took me on two thirty-mile walks. 'For a tall man,' he remarked, as I struggled to keep up with his vast stride (he was six foot one to my six feet), 'you take very short steps.' 'Now that I think of it,' I replied, 'I believe you're right. Margaret's not quite five feet; I've got used down the years to holding back to her speed.'

Our tiny cottage was at the foot of lovely Mount Errigal, the setting at a later date for my book *Brigid and the Mountain*. The merciless Noel insisted on climbing the mountain, this time accompanied by the three of us. What with the loose scree, it was almost as tiring coming down as going up. Later, on our return to Dublin, Margaret held for him a one-man exhibition of his Mayo and Donegal photographs. Later again his wife Margot and he parted, Margot, who was Scottish, vanishing to India where she adopted Indian dress and customs.

Margaret also held an exhibition for our President, the President of the Royal Hibernian Academy Dermod O'Brien. The twenty-two pictures were advertised in *Commentary* as 'A representative collection, including new work.' They consisted of landscapes for the most part, but there was a portrait of the poet George Russell ('AE'), done in 1914.

The exhibition was opened by the distinguished actor and director of the Dublin Gate Theatre Company, Hilton Edwards. This man, accustomed to appearing before four hundred or so people at the Gate Theatre, and perhaps three times that number at the Gaiety, not to mention theatres in London and abroad, confessed to me that he felt extremely nervous before the fifty or so assembled in the gallery. 'It's the fact of talking about art to all these distinguished artists,' he said. (Jack B. Yeats, the great Irish Impressionist, was in the audience.) 'Are you nervous at a first-night in the theatre?' I asked. 'Yes, but I can throw myself into a sort of neutral gear.' What did it signify to him, the matter of mere numbers? A sensitive and brilliant man, he thought only in terms of the intellectual quality of those who waited on his words.

Dermod O'Brien was born at Mount Trenchard, the home of his uncle, the second Lord Monteagle. At first he spent most of his time in Ireland and England; in England at Harrow and Cambridge, his holidays in Ireland with Charlotte Grace O'Brien, of whom Stephen Gwynn wrote a biography.

On leaving Cambridge, he went to Antwerp to study art. He regretted not having started earlier; he felt that unless one began young one could never become a master of line. At Antwerp he often played the cello with his friends. His step-mother was a very good pianist and a close friend of Jenny Lynd. From Antwerp he went to Paris where he met Sir William Rothenstein. Then it was London, where he began his career as a portrait painter. He became acquainted with Henry Tonks, McColl, Steer, and that great stylist the Irish novelist and short-story writer George Moore.

Tonks and Steer were looking for fresh lodgings and a room-mate with whom to share them. Both their choices fell on Dermod O'Brien. He said that he would lodge with whichever of them found rooms first. Tonks won. An ascetic and irritable man, Tonks couldn't stand noise. So he put down a thick carpet in Dermod O'Brien's room overhead. Tonks was an early bed-goer, but Dermod liked going out to parties. So another thick carpet went down on the stairs. 'You were in late last night,' said Tonks. 'I couldn't get to sleep.' 'But,' protested Dermod O'Brien, 'I tried not to make any noise. Did you hear me come in?' 'No,' said Tonks gloomily. 'That's why I couldn't get to sleep.'

Equipped with the experience gained from his studies in Paris, Dermod O'Brien adopted the 'plein air' canon in his landscapes to render the light and colour of the County Limerick countryside. In 1907 he had become an Associate of the Royal Hibernian Academy, the following year a full member, and two years later President. When George Moore came to Ireland to link up with W. B. Yeats on the literary side of the Irish Renaissance, he remarked that the artistic side might safely be left in the hands of George Osbourne and Dermod O'Brien.

The portrait that Dermod O'Brien painted of my mother, Nora Dorman, was exhibited at the Royal Academy in London in 1929. He also painted two portraits of my uncle Lennox Robinson, both being produced at the same time, one of which hung in Galway and the other in the Peacock Theatre in Dublin. His portrait of Lord Cloncurry for the Kildare Street Club in Dublin was considered by many to be the best portrait of its year at the Academy. He exhibited with George Russell ('AE') two or three times around 1914 at the Mills Hall.

After a one-man exhibition by Richard Pearsall, opened by Dermod O'Brien, Margaret held an impromptu showing in the second gallery of pictures by Maurice McGonigal, RHA. It came about thus. She was, as usual, using the second gallery to display a selection of the pictures being offered for hire or sale. Among these was one of three Connemara women by Maurice McGonigal priced at something like sixty-five guineas. A priest appeared and suddenly flashed before our eyes a fifty-pound bank note saying, 'If you will sell me that picture right now on the spot, I'll give you this fifty-pound note for it.' It would be rather like, in these days of a devalued currency, flashing before the eyes of a young couple of small means a two or three hundred pound note.

The man of God, plainly versed not only in the ways of the next world but also of this, doubtless had discovered that the combined visual force of a huge bank note, coupled with the ultimatum that the sale must be immediate (no time for second thoughts or consultation with the artist) worked. It certainly worked with us. We simply could not get in touch with Maurice McGonical on the spot, and we simply could not let that fifty-pound note walk out of the door. Short of holding up the priest at the point of a paint brush, or coshing him over the head with a still-life in oils, there was no way that we could have prevented his escape. We said yes. The fifty-pound note was ours or, rather, Maurice McGonical's less our commission.

When we later showed him the note, expecting him to be delighted, we were dashed to see that he was far from that. Of course he was down some fifteen pounds on the deal, and it was he who had put in the hard graft of making the picture. Also, we didn't know what prices he was used to getting. To mollify him, Margaret offereed to turn over the entire reserve gallery to his work for a month. I don't think that he could have been too disappointed with the fifty-pound note, for he at once agreed.

He had begun his career as a worker in stained glass. A scholarship secured at the College of Art led him to study painting. He won the Taylor Scholarship in 1924, and in 1927 went to study in Holland. In 1938 he was appointed assistant professor of painting at the National College of Art.

He brought along half a dozen paintings and drawings. All of them, to our momentary surprise, were preliminary studies for his painting of the Connemara women. A write-up of this mini-exhibition appeared in one or two of the Dublin newspapers. Suddenly the priest was in the room again. His brow bore a thunder cloud. 'All these copies of his — his Three Graces!' he exploded. He started a number of further protests which always faded away in his throat. What could he say? It was not only a time-honoured but often extremely necessary practice for an artist to make preliminary notes and studies for the main work. All the pictures, studies as well as finished product, were the original conception and execution of the artist. The priest, still quietly erupting, departed to rejoin company with what he plainly considered to be his devalued purchase. As to the studies, Margaret had sold five out of the six of them in a few days, and Maurice McGonigal had to ferry in more pictures.

Some time during April or May 1942 we closed down Picture Hire. It had been a gallery full of animation, full of pictures and full of people, in short, apparently highly prosperous. But our average weekly profits had been about one pound and ten shillings (£1.50)! In any case the proprietor of the art shop downstairs wanted his two rooms back. Many of those who had been most generous of their advice as to how we ought to run the gallery, now raised their voices to urge us to continue elsewhere. When we invited them to join us as co-directors of such a venture, and mentioned the one pound and ten shillings, the silence that followed could be clearly heard from Lower Baggott Street down as far as the end of O'Connell Street, the Gate Theatre, and the Municipal Gallery, beyond which all culture ceases.

In those days there was a garden square (now developed into a memorial to Irish political martyrs), just beyond the Gate Theatre, on the far side of it Findlater's Church. The southern approaches to the city I know, from Uncle Tom's various residences at different times at Shankhill or Glencullen or Ballycorus Road; and from Uncle Lennox's at Foxrock or Dalkey or Monkstown. But what becomes of Dublin beyond Findlater's Church and the Municipal Gallery I have to idea. No doubt it fades away gradually into a region of primal mist — wreathed swamps, probably inhabited by demons and dragons.

With the ruthlessness of youth, and giving the artists scant time to collect their pictures, Margaret and I had closed the gallery almost with a bang. Her chief interest now lay in producing a baby, and mine in producing a magazine. Dermod O'Brien said to me crossly, 'Many of the artists only came to you because of my name.'

A little later, Margaret and I were in a box at the Gaiety Theatre. We got complimentary tickets on my card as editor of my monthly magazine, *Commentary*. In a box opposite I saw Uncle Lennox. During the first interval, I made my way round to greet him. He immediately began, in front of some ladies, to upbraid me for closing the gallery so abruptly. 'I know,' he said with a contemptuous inflexion, 'that you're having a baby.' Our son Paul was on the way. 'Now, now, Lennox!' intervened one of the ladies. I smiled, bowed slightly, and left.

AFTERTHOUGHT

The story of the manner of Kenneth Hall's suicide was put around Dublin at the time by, I can only suppose, Basil Rakoczi. Very many years later, I received a letter from Dr Brian Kennedy, Curator of Twentieth Century Art at the Ulster Museum in Belfast, who has done so much to preserve and further the reputations of artists working in Ireland. He had read my book, *My Uncle Lennox*; and also had perused, in the library of Dublin University, the issues of my monthly magazine, *Commentary*. Tactfully, he hinted to me that

I had got the Kenneth Hall story wrong. When I set out to write *Portrait of My Youth*, an improved and extended version of *My Uncle Lennox*, I remembered this.

I asked him for the truth. I cannot do better than paraphrase his reply. In April 1939, in London, Kenneth Hall had an operation for mastoiditis. It was not entirely successful, and the ailment plagued him for the rest of his life. During February–March 1945 he had a lengthy stay in the Adelaide Hospital, Dublin. There he was again treated for mastoiditis, but left feeling little the better. In September 1945 he returned to London, hoping to get better treatment there. He was also treated at this time for acute depression, to which he had always been prone. By early summer, 1946, his depression had grown worse. He was obsessed with the idea that he suffered from cancer. Also, he had certain relationship troubles with family and friends. On the twenty-sixth of July he took his own life through an overdose of barbiturates. A post-mortem revealed no physical illness. His funeral was to Golders Green Crematorium on 31 July.

Chapter Eight
John Betjeman's Braces

On November the tenth, 1941, a report appeared in the Dublin *Evening Mail* which read, '*Commentary*, the new sixpenny magazine, of which the first issue appeared this month, is run in conjunction with the Picture Hire Club at 24 Molesworth Street, and is edited by Sean Dorman. This enterprising monthly is certain to be welcomed by all art and drama lovers in Ireland. Contributors to the November issue include Lennox Robinson and Mainie Jellett. Subsequent issues will carry articles by such personalities as Jack B. Yeats, Dermod O'Brien, Hilton Edwards, Henri Silvy, and others well-known in the world of art and the theatre.'

For our various one-man exhibitions, my wife Margaret and I had been getting our catalogues printed by the Spartan Printing Company at 65 South William Street, Dublin. On one occasion the catalogue was late, the exhibition was due to open in a few hours, and I walked to the printer's in a considerable anxiety. Ascending the narrow staircase, I entered the small room. Behind the counter I found the printer standing at his pedal machine. As I watched him finishing off our order, the yearning that I had long felt inside me burst out. 'I've always wanted to have a magazine of my own.' Instantly he replied, 'So have I.' *Commentary* was born.

Tom Hosgood was not a literary man. He was not, primarily, even a printer. His degree was in science. But he had emerged from university at a moment when scientists were in small demand in Ireland. So he rented an office, paid for his small machine by instalments, and printed catalogues, leaflets and the like, picking out the metal letters from their pigeon-holes with a pair of tweezers and setting up a page of print within the frame of a chase. That was all right for a small catalogue, or for headlines, advertisements, captions under pictures. But imagine setting up type, the letters sought for and picked out one by one, for a solid page of printing! Few would so much as have considered the idea. It was a job in those days for a monotype or linotype machine. For Tom Hosgood, it was a long day's work just to set up half a page, and by the time he closed his office he sometimes could hardly see straight. We had brought out a preliminary leaflet announcing the contents of the October issue. When the moment came to put the leaflet on show at the entrance to our galleries, we had to cross out the word 'October' and substitute 'November'.

Pessimistically I suggested to Tom Hosgood that we might not be able to sell at Picture Hire more than a hundred copies of the magazine. He maintained that we should be able to dispose of at least two hundred and fifty. He was right. At the end of the December issue appeared a triumphant note, 'SOLD OUT! The November issue of *Commentary* was completely sold out long before the month was up. We are printing twice as many copies of the December issue. But,' we added with a touch of canny salesmanship, 'to make sure of your copy complete the form on page 4 *TODAY*.' In the end we decided not to risk quite doubling the number, and Tom Hosgood ran off four hundred copies. *The Irish Times* carried a notice of our first issue. '*Commentary*, the organ of the Picture Hire Club, is concerned with the affairs of art, artists and art lovers. Lennox Robinson and Sean Dorman contribute short stories, T. N. Hosgood talks about *Colour*, Mainie Jellett discusses *Art as a Spiritual Force*, there is also a sketch of the career and work of Dermod O'Brien.'

My first love then was the stage. I was determined to develop *Commentary* into a theatre magazine, with painting holding the second place. It would be truer to say that painting was to hold the third place, theatre the second, and my own writing the first. But, at the time, I kept my lips buttoned about this last! I set about making my name as well known as might be, not only by printing it more prominently as the magazine grew in presence and circulation, but also by finally attaching a photograph to it. When I did eventually open my lips on the subject four years later in my Christmas 1945 issue, in response to a press attack, I opened them most roundly.

The attack on me appeared in *The Standard*, a journal which was more or less the mouthpiece of the Catholic Church in Ireland. I had written a couple of editorials on my notions about marriage. *The Standard* took exception to them. Their writer didn't just stick to his thesis, but raked everything into the battle. 'I think,' he wrote, 'I should know this young man if I ever met him in the street, not from the definiteness of any opinions expressed, but from the size of the photograph of himself with which, with the instinct of the true artist, he has filled one quarter of the area of the front page . . . As somebody said somewhere, *Commentary is superfluous*.' (It was actually written by Myles na Copaleen in the *Irish Times*.)

In a long reply I set about the writer, who had sniped from behind the pen-name of 'Pat Murphy', dealing with all the points he had raised. On the subject of the photograph I wrote, 'If he will turn over the leaves and look at other pages, he will see that even larger photographs adorn them. I like large photographs. I think that they are more effective than small photographs. I like large, bold, generous effects. Certainly my photograph occupies a quarter of the area of my first page. It was carefully designed to do so. And the title is given another quarter, and the two columns of text the last two quarters. The lay-out was designed on a geometrical principle of quarters. Only, as such a pattern would, like Mr. Murphy's irony, have been too simple and obvious, it was given a little subtlety and variety by the device of "bleeding off", that is, the photograph was carried up to the neighbouring edges of the page.

'As to my printing a photograph of myself at all, as an author I certainly do not seek obscurity. It has always been a source of bitter disappointment to me that I have never been able to afford to have erected, at the summit of one of the taller buildings in the immediate neighbourhood of O'Connell Bridge, a sky-sign in multi-coloured neon lights, flashing out my name every ten seconds in letters some twelve feet high. Firms advertise themselves, and an author is a one-man firm. If you do not put up your own neon signs, it is pretty certain that (except in the long run, and it may be a very long run, and you may be dead first) no one else will put them up for you. Good work that is not advertised does not bring fame. Alternatively, of course, mere publicity, without true good work attached to it, is not fame either; it is merely notoriety. But I am a good writer, and shall be better hereafter.'

Shortly after this, Jimmy O'Dea, then Ireland's leading stage comic, indeed an artist of genius, whose pantomimes and revues regularly had the longest runs in Dublin (he also had his own programme on BBC radio), approached me in the Gaiety Theatre. He congratulated me on my article and sympathised with my desire to have my name incorporated into the Dublin skyline. I wasn't surprised. He had his own name large enough on his posters! If anyone got too big for his boots at one of his rehearsals, he quickly cut him down to size with the reminder, 'It's me that they come to see.' There was no reply to that. They did.

It emerged that he himself had fallen foul of *The Standard*; quite how, remained obscure. Perhaps some of his jokes had got too 'blue'. An actor once remarked to me, 'In Holy Ireland no one is allowed to make sex jokes, so Jimmy O'Dea has to go for his to the lavatory.' Of course this was an overstatement. Given that good script on which the majority of even the most outstanding comics depend, he extracted every last nuance out of it and dominated the stage. But fancy a popular comedian, in times of trouble when scripts ran thin, not being allowed to make sex jokes! It's like telling a beautiful woman at a party that she mustn't take her dress off, or a horse that it must give up eating oats.

Ever since Uncle Tom and Aunt Ethel had taken my sisters and me as children to our first pantomime, I had seen Jimmy O'Dea only on the stage and as the funny man. Through force of habit I found myself receiving every perfectly serious remark that he made with laughter or at least a smirk. Finally he said with a smile, 'I know — the stage comic!' That pulled me up. Once, during the second interval of one of Uncle Lennox's funniest comedies at the Abbey Theatre, two American girls approached him in the foyer for his autograph. Everything that he said to them evoked peals of helpless laughter. I think that if he had offered them a cup of coffee, they would have died of mirth. He was a great 'mixer' and took it all in his stride. His eyebrows raised quizzically, he kept shooting smiles of comic helplessness in my direction. But to return to Jimmy O'Dea. When I offered him a drink, he said that he would have a ginger beer. His doctor had told him that he must keep away from whisky or he would kill himself. When at a later time I sadly heard of his death, I wondered if he had returned to his whisky in the end.

But all this is four years on. Before that, *Commentary* had still to make its way through its early stages. In the 1942 January issue appeared another triumphant note, 'SOLD OUT AGAIN! We sold so fast in November that we printed an almost double issue for December.' (The figure, as already said, was four hundred.) 'We sold that too, so here is a yet bigger January issue' (actually, six hundred and twenty-five). Although the greatest labour for Tom Hosgood remained the type-setting, nevertheless, coming on top of it, this necessity to run off every sheet six hundred and twenty-five times, as compared with the original two hundred and fifty, was beginning to make itself felt. When the figure was lifted to seven hundred and fifty for the February issue, this, together with a feverish cold, proved too much for the gallant Tom, and we had to label the issue, 'February-March'. I myself was doing all the editing, lay-out and make-up, and securing through my connections contributions from well-known people.

Coming as did this issue at the time of the closing down of the Picture Hire Club, we could no longer decorate the top of our editorial page with the names of our distinguished President and Vice-Presidents, under which our little known names had sheltered. The page, by comparison, looked bleak indeed with just: Editor, Sean Dorman; Production Manager (a grand title, this!), T. N. Hosgood; Publicity Manager, Edith Crook (Tom's fiancee); Editor of Art Notes, Margaret Dorman. It was a daunting prospect thus to issue out into a cold world, with no longer any gallery in which to display and sell our wares. Yet for me there was exhilaration too. With pictures no longer under my arm to cause me to be taken for one of those goddam artists, I was unequivocally a writer at last! As to selling the magazine, I found five bookshops and three other firms willing to display and dispose of copies on commission.

The great Irish painter Jack B. Yeats, brother of the equally great Irish poet W. B. Yeats, had sent us a short story, rather an episode than a story, called *A Fast Trotting Mare*, for our second issue. It was a long episode. As time ran out and Tom Hosgood struggled with his letter by letter setting up of the print, I cavalierly and without prior consultation with the author cut the script severely. Jack B. Yeats's great reputation as an artist had made me regard his writing as a mere by-the-way pastime. I later discovered that he published quite a lot. But I most certainly found the script dull, and was having it printed solely for the sake of getting his name on to our cover! He was offended by the cuts. I made my lame excuses. He sent us nothing more.

About a year later he approached me in his floppy clothes and invited me round to his studio. His appearance and manner reminded me strongly of his brother, W. B. Yeats. 'I have a very few colours on my pallette,' he said, exhibiting it to me. 'Before I admit a new colour, it has to grow on me and become part of me.' In July 1943 Dr. Theodore Goodman, who had become my art critic, wrote, 'Jack B. Yeats is the most distinguished of living Irish artists. He has been accorded the almost unique distinction of a one-man show in the London National Gallery, and he is equally well known in America. Only time can show if the work of Yeats will rank with the great Impressionists of other countries, but he must always take an important place as an artist who has rendered the same service to Irish painting as his brother did to Irish poetry.' Just recently, so very many years later, I re-read *A Fast Trotting Mare*. I found it knowledgeable, intimately felt — and still dull!

In the April 1942 issue of *Commentary* appeared the triumphant note, 'WE SOLD OUT our last two issues and our circulation now ranks above that of a number of well-known Dublin literary periodicals. Make sure of your copy by placing a regular order.' No mention of which periodicals or how we knew what their circulations were! Perhaps just a piece of sharp salesmanship in the blessed days before the Trade Descriptions Act! Our own circulation was now eight hundred and seventy-five copies. Tom Hosgood, as I hovered in his office on edge to get out the issue, had to ask me to run off some fifty sheets while he set up the last of the print. I had great difficulty at first in setting down straight each sheet on to the metal 'table' while, under the compulsion of my one-footed pedalling, the printing arm rhythmically descended upon the blank paper to stamp out its chase — full of text. By the May 1942 issue, with its twelve hundred and fifty copies, Tom was at his last gasp, and I had to resign myself to giving up part of my writing time in order to appear fairly regularly at the printing office to run off sheets.

Tom Hosgood and his fiancee had long been waiting until they could afford to get married. Neither the printing of catalogues nor the production of *Commentary* seemed at all likely to accomplish this. If Ireland had then small need of scientists, a Britain locked in the Second World War had every need. Tom Hosgood secured a post in an English munitions factory. With all the takings of the magazine henceforward coming to me alone, I was able to afford to transfer the production of the fifteen hundred copies of the June issue to the large and well equipped Sackville Press at 11 to 13 Findlater Place, off O'Connell Street.

I also, in exchange for giving half-page advertisements, was allowed to sell in the foyers of the Gaiety, Olympia and Gate Theatres. This I did through a horde of small boys more or less controlled by a larger boy. They had to account to him for all the monies (sixpence a copy) that they took, were allowed to keep a penny a copy for themselves, and he retained a halfpenny a copy for overseeing them. So I received four pence halfpenny on each copy. It was an uneasy existence. The boys would sometimes overstep the mark in pressing for sales and pester the theatres' clientele. Or they would allow them to suppose that the magazine was a theatre programme. There would be a complaint from the management, and a request that the boys be kept under a better control. This was quite impossible; I couldn't be out night after night patrolling the foyers of three Dublin theatres, not to mention the pavements outside. Yet the managements, though they might make ominous sounds, never asked me to go. There was not only their free advertising space, but also in every issue criticisms of, and advance notices on, their productions.

When I finally did withdraw and start selling through the newsagents, it was my own decision. Indeed John Daly, the manager of the Opera House in Cork where I also sold, expressed his disappointment at the change. As the wholesalers took for themselves a penny a copy, and the retailers a further penny halfpenny, I now got only threepence halfpenny. But life became much more settled. In these present days of seemingly never- ending inflation it is hard to credit that *Commentary* came out selling at sixpence and, five and a half years later when it closed down, was still selling at the same price. When the magazine grew to its largest, though most certainly not to its best, its circulation was possibly (I have no note of it) about three thousand copies monthly. There was only a small population to sell to, and we covered minority interests by and large. With the end of the war and the return of better paper supplies, the newspapers and the women's magazines were able to reinflate to their previous sizes, to suck away most of the advertising from the smaller publications, and *Commentary* was doomed.

But, before that, it was destined to pass a lively five and a half years with some of the best known names in the theatre and concert hall, Irish and otherwise, passing through its pages. Its liveliness derived too I feel, at least in a small way, from the iconoclasm of a young man's mind — my own. The two idols at which I delighted to swing my hammer were the medical profession and, more especially, the Irish book censorship as then applied. Uneasy lest I might, in my green pugnacity, have overstated my case and stumbled into folly, I have recently consulted some early copies of *Commentary* with a view to making excuses. But I found that my younger self had comported himself with rather more credit than I supposed, had blundered into aggressive overstatements rather less than I feared, and that there was a certain exhilaration to be found in the whirlwind assaults of springtime vigour. So I shall make no retractions here. Rather do I hope to publish some of the early essays, together with new, in another book.* There I can make such reservations as I feel I should.

My wife Margaret's and my first theatrical contact in Dublin was with the then Lord Longford's company. She and I haunted the empty auditorium of the Gate Theatre during the rehearsals of a most original production of *Romeo and Juliet* by Lord Longford's director, John Izon. Finally we were noticed sufficiently to scrape an acquaintance with John Izon and his wife Phyllis. They took their place among our best friends, and through them we got to know other members of the cast. Later followed an invitation to me from Lord Longford to write a burlesque of his current production of Chekhov's *The Three Sisters*. The burlesque was given three performances, to raise money for the Gate Theatre, in a large marquee in the grounds of the Earl's town house.

John Izon had played walk-on parts with Frank Benson's Shakespeare Company at the age of nineteen. At Oxford he joined the

'Physicians, Priests and Physicists', published 1993.

Oxford University Dramatic Society. Although himself at New College, he directed for Christchurch Kyd's *Spanish Tragedy* and Marlowe's *Edward II*. He was apprenticed to Hans Strohbach, director at the Cologne and Dresden Opera Houses. His first professional job was as an actor and assistant director at the Festival Theatre, Cambridge. He worked for a season as stage manager at the Old Vic and Sadlers Wells, and stage-managed for Nancy Price. He acted and directed for the Oxford Rep., and also for Baxter Somerville of the Croydon Rep. After a brief experience of management on his own, he joined Longford Productions. He contributed many articles to *Commentary*.

The fund-raising burlesque and garden fete was followed by a dance at the Earl's town residence (his country residence was in County Westmeath). Margaret and I were invited. As Lady Longford bade us goodbye she said, 'Thank you for coming and drinking our bad champagne.' I couldn't think what to reply, so simply melted away into the night simpering inanely.

To swing back in time, and to England, for a moment, in 1936 Lord Longford had staged his Chinese play, *Armlet of Jade*, at the Westminster Theatre in London. The cast was drawn mostly from the Dublin Abbey and Gate Theatres. I had sent reports of its success to *The Irish Times* and the *Irish Press*. In the cast was Denis Johnston, author of the plays *The Moon in the Yellow River* and *The Old Lady Says No!* He and his then wife Shelah Richards, the Abbey Theatre actress, who also later directed and had her own company, gave a party at their home in Barnes. The party was largely devoted to discussing the press notices. The Abbey actress, and later stage director, Ria Mooney took me to it. Lord and Lady Longford, who herself wrote a number of plays for the Gate Theatre and published books, were of course there. So also was the young Irish starlet, Geraldine Fitzgerald. She was then working for a British film company at ninety pounds a week, when a pound really was worth a pound. (I myself at that time was living on three pounds a week!) She later secured a Hollywood contract.

I continued to cover, in a free-lance capacity for the same two Dublin papers, Lord Longford's success with Eugene O'Neill's *Ah, Wilderness!* He had given this play its European premiere at the

Dublin Gate Theatre. Following on *Armlet of Jade*, he staged *Ah, Wilderness!* at the Westminster Theatre for two weeks. At the final matinee I found myself seated close to Bernard Shaw, who appeared to be absorbed in the play. It was then transferred to the West End. After its first week at the Ambassadors' Theatre, Fred Johnson returned to the Abbey, and his role of 'Nat Miller' was taken over by Paul Farrell. At the Ambassadors' three years earlier Paul Farrell had had a resounding success in my Uncle Lennox Robinson's comedy, *Is Life Worth Living?* (*Drama at Inish*, to give it its Abbey Theatre title), which ran for over a hundred performances. After more than fifty performances of O'Neill's play at the Ambassadors', Lord Longford took his company back to the Westminster Theatre to give Denis Johnston's *Bride for the Unicorn* its premiere. Some of the backcloths were designed by the well-known Irish artist Norah McGuinness. Denis Johnston's *Storm Song* was also staged at the Embassy Theatre, with his wife-to-be, Betty Chancellor, in the cast.

Shortly after drinking the Earl and Countess of Longford's allegedly bad champagne, Margaret and I asked them and the Longford Players to tea at our flat on Clontarf. Virtually the whole of the Company, 'liegemen to the Earl' as they called themselves, turned up. Lord and Lady Longford brought with them John Betjeman, now alas the late Poet Laureate Sir John Betjeman. He was charming, amusing, and self-effacing — apart from the matter of his dress. As, on arrival, he cast off his dark cloak, there was a brief flash from its crimson lining. Carefully folding the once more sober cloak and placing it over the back of a chair, he unbuttoned his jacket for a moment before buttoning it up again. But that moment had revealed a pair of braces covered with pictures of bosomy mermaids. These braces stole the show. He was constantly pestered to unbutton his jacket and show them off. Finally, with immense good humour, he left his jacket permanently open and, as we munched our scones, sandwiches and cakes, and drank our tea, we were able to feast our eyes too.

John Betjeman with *Lord* Longford! I had heard tell that, in his wish to leave behind the bourgeois world in which he had been brought up, he had to a degree chased after titles. However, conscious of his own powers, he always expected to be treated as an equal. He had a special liking for Irish peers because, he said, they were so *dotty*. While at Oxford, he used to spend the university vacations at the Clandeboye mansion of the Marquess of Dufferin and Ava in Ulster. But he felt at home with all the members of the Anglo-Irish Ascendancy, whether north or south of 'The Border'.

Noting, at the time, that John Betjeman, Lord Longford, and Longford's stage director John Izon, had all been up at Oxford, I vaguely supposed that they might have become acquainted there. Had I been a more social animal, doubtless I should have discovered. But I tended to be aloof, for the most part buried in my family, my writing, and the monthly production of my magazine. Yet I remember having the feeling that Betjeman and Longford were of a somewhat older generation than John Izon, his wife Phyllis, Margaret, and myself. I have since discovered that, at least in the case of Betjeman, this was so. Betjeman went up to Magdalen College in 1925, whereas my dates at Worcester College were 1930 to 1934 (though my *matriculation* date is given in the records as 1929).

As Lord Longford was at Christ Church, that college-collector of titles, would not John Betjeman, that personal collector of titles, have perhaps dug him out if they were up at the same time? However, Magdalen too was not without power in that respect. When I was up, it was able to boast among its undergraduates the then Prince of Wales. As to John Izon, it was he who told me that Lord Longford had been at Christ Church. There, the Earl had thrown his considerable physical weight around as an Irish nationalist. At length some of his fellow undergraduates had lifted up 'that bloody Irishman' and deposited him into the artificial pond in the centre of the quadrangle. It must have been quite a splash! This does not necessarily mean that Longford and Izon met when the latter was directing the plays of Kyd and Marlowe for Christ Church. Longford may have told Izon the story later in Dublin.

Like Izon, John Betjeman had become a member of the Oxford University Dramatic Society (the OUDS). His membership did not long endure. Taking up a photograph of a rehearsal at the OUDS, he attached an irreverent caption to it — and was asked to leave. Others of his adventures strike a sympathetic chord within me. He spent lavishly on clothes (hence, doubtless, the dashing cloak with the crimson lining at our Dublin tea party). I hadn't the resources to undertake that, except in one respect only. My idol at that time was the English musical comedy star, Jack Buchanan. No matter what the cost, I *must* have a suit of 'tails' the equal of his. I consulted my room-mate, Robert Talbot. After two years in rooms at, respectively, Worcester and Keble, we now were together in University licensed digs. He advised me most earnestly to apply to Hall Bros, then accredited to the Prince of Wales. 'You wear,' he assured me, 'clothes acquired from Hall Bros inside out to show the label.' The tailor called at our address to take the necessary measurements. What material did I want? I had only one answer — 'the best.' What cloth for the lapels? 'The best.' What back and sleeve buttons? 'The best.'

Betjeman decided to read English, but found Anglo-Saxon too much for him. I, also, found it quite appalling. But I have already expressed, in an earlier chapter, my feelings vis-a-vis the English courses then on offer. He ran up huge bills at Basil Blackwell's bookshop, bills which he was able to settle only on the death of his father some four or five years later. I, too, found the second-hand department (books of past periods) all but irresistible. But I was able, just, to keep abreast of my large, though doubtless less large, purchases. In relation to such debts at Oxford, some years later I overheard a most enlightening conversation. I had returned very belatedly to have my MA conferred. My means were small, and I took a 'bed and breakfast' at a cheap hotel near the station. The lounge was filled with travelling salesmen. One of them remarked to his fellows that though the debts run up by the students were enormous, the bad debts were extremely few. Nearly all were settled within a year or two by their families.

Abandoning English, Betjeman set out to acquire a degree in Welsh. In this he failed, and also in the then compulsory Divinity Moderations. As a result, he was sent down. He took a kind of revenge by delighting in the fact that Magdalen College had had to endure the expense of importing, twice a week from Aberystwith University in Wales, a tutor to coach him.

He approached the redoubtable Gabbitas, Thring and Company, known to all schoolmasters, to find him a post in teaching. How often, after I had been obliged to close down my magazine *Commentary*, did I not approach them too! Later I preferred to advertise in *The Times Educational Supplement*. I at least had a BA, later boosted to MA, and could secure positions teaching English, until I managed to shift over into much preferred French with supporting German. But Betjeman, without a degree, was pushed into coaching cricket, about which he knew almost nothing. He soon escaped into writing prestigious articles on architecture, whereas I was doomed to teach for twenty-six years. However, during that time I was able to struggle with re-writing after re-writing of a novel, much later published by my own Raffeen Press under the title of *Red Roses for Jenny*. I also had set up, in 1957, with an ever-shifting membership of about thirty, the Sean Dorman Manuscript Society for mutual criticism; a society still being run by others, under the same title, thirty-five years later as I pen these lines. My magazine *Writing* also was founded shortly afterwards, in 1959, and sold only after twenty-six years of continuous publication.

While working for *The Architectural Review*, John Betjeman met and married, in 1933, Penelope Chetwode. Chetwode! How that name carries me back to memories of my parents telling me that only the Viceroy, the Commander-in-Chief, and some Maharajah or other, were allowed to drive a car above Simla, because of the danger to horsemen on the narrow Himalayan road. Penelope, the daughter of that same mysterious Commander-in-Chief, Field Marshal Lord Chetwode! I have, not so long ago, seen a film of Penelope Chetwode and her explorations in the Himalayas, seeking out Hindu temples.

When I met John Betjaman in Dublin, I had no idea that his wife was over too, or that he had children. I knew only that he was Press Attaché to the British Embassy, or High Commission. Also that he was acquainted with Geoffrey Taylor, Poetry Editor to *The Bell*, run by Sean O'Faolain and Frank O'Connor. This literary magazine was, together with the *Irish Times* (and my own *Commentary*), about the only publication to challenge the stifling censorship being imposed, in effect, by the Catholic Church in Ireland. This literary censorship was intensified by the political censorship on radio and the press, supposedly for the sole purpose of preserving the Irish Republic's neutrality during the Second World War. But when a homosexual scandal became manifest in a Catholic seminary, the political censorship was used to block the reporting of it. In protest, Sean O'Faolain and Frank O'Connor produced a *Letter to the Minister of Justice*. This got as far as being set up in galley proof, and a copy of it was sent to me as editor of *Commentary*. But the 'letter' got no further. The printers of *The Bell*, I was told, also had as a client a large Catholic publication, and they refused to set up the letter in page form. As to *The Bell*, I believe that someone had given a thousand pounds, then a large sum, to finance it. When the thousand pounds ran out, *The Bell* perforce had to close.

Concerning Betjeman's wife and children, I learnt only much later that the marriage was an unusual one. He regarded the children as his wife's rather than his, and husband and wife very much followed their own paths. In Dublin, Betjeman once again identified with the Anglo-Irish, joining their Kildare Street Club. Yet he also ably assisted his Ambassador, or High Commissioner, Sir John Maffey. It was a delicate task to marry the promotion of Britain's point of view with a due regard for Ireland's neutrality. Always, but always, the sharpest watch on every move was maintained from the German Embassy.

My Uncle Lennox Robinson had, under the title of *Roly-Poly*, written a theatrical adaptation of Guy de Maupassant's famous story, *Boule de Suif*, in which some German officers appear to poor advantage. Uncle Lennox told me that the actress and producer, Shelah Richards, had said that the play was 'under written'. 'Which,' he added with a self-pleased smile, 'is a very nice thing to say.' I made no reply. For the honour of art, I dislike writers or any other artists diminishing themselves by showing the smallest tendency to lap up flattery, rather than to dig for the truth. After I had seen the play, I couldn't but feel that Shelah Richards' 'under written' should be translated into 'very poor'. Very poor or not, Lennox Robinson's great reputation in Dublin meant that it could be staged. Hilton Edwards and Micheal MacLiammoir, directors of Gate Theatre Productions, did so at the Gate Theatre.

Almost at once came a protest from the German Embassy. The Irish Government, acting under the powers conferred upon it by the political censorship, at the last moment forbad the show to take place. The Gate Theatre was filled with a first-night audience. While the Act gave the Government powers to prevent a public performance, they had none to prevent a private one. Uncle Lennox, impecunious because of his drinking despite his royalties from many

107

quarters, stepped forward on to the stage. He announced that everyone would have his money returned to him. He, Lennox Robinson, would buy up all the seats in the house. Hilton Edwards, who was directing the play, was heard to mutter, 'With what?'

After the performance, the story was current in Dublin that the Military Attaché, or some other, at the German Embassy had challenged Lennox Robinson to a duel. The idea of Uncle Lennox, tall, droopy and short-sighted, fighting a duel, was not without its comic aspect. Neither I nor, I suspect, anyone else, heard any more of the matter.

As to the Clontarf tea party, next day we learnt from one of the Longford Company that, before coming to tea with us, Lord Longford had already taken tea at the Country Shop in St Stephen's Green and that, after leaving us, he had a further tea. This was no reflection on our hospitality, our informant assured us. It was the custom of the Earl to eat almost non-stop. Indeed he himself had remarked at our flat, as he sucked a piece of icing off his finger, 'They tell me that I eat too much.'

Of medium height, he was nearly as rotund as G K Chesterton, whom I once heard as a guest speaker at the Oxford Union. 'It will come as a surprise to this House to learn,' said Chesterton in his rather squeaky voice, 'that I never had any ambitions to be a cat burglar.'

The only other person that I have met more rotund than Lord Longford was a man in Paris. Uncle Lennox had given me a letter of introduction to a young American poet whose name I forget. The poet and his wife took me to see this man. The picture that has stuck in my memory is of a single-storey shack with a corrugated-iron roof. Presumably even in a city as beautifully built as Paris there can be such a thing. The huge figure reclined on a couch at the far end of the room. He was ministered to by a mostly silent dark haired slip of a girl. He received me with the utmost courtesy, but excused himself from rising. It would have been a major undertaking. Who was the man? The name that emerges through the mists of memory is — Ford Maddox Ford.

Not so long after Lord Longford had taken tea with us, I was told that he was in hospital with a boil on his bottom. Not of course a dignified disease. But any disposition on my part to smirk was inhibited by my own painful memories. At my preparatory school, Castle Park at Dalkey, Dublin, I had myself been smitten with such an outbreak at a not dissimilar location. Daily I bent forward while that devoted matron, Miss Webster, ministered to my miseries. The Earl duly recovered. My own theory then, before I was told that a boil was considered to be an external infection into a hair follicle, was that his illness was due to his excessive eating, and not to any ingredients in our sandwiches, or even to the shock of John Betjeman's braces.

Chapter Nine
My Uncle Lennox

Was it my Uncle Lennox's fault or mine that, at the age of twenty-nine, I threw T. S. Eliot's manuscript on to the floor? You may say that it was a childish act on my part. But I should reply that it wasn't a carefully thought out act; it all took place in a split second, almost as a reflex action. And, anyway, I didn't know that the manuscript was T. S. Eliot's. I thought it was Uncle Lennox's.

But why, you may riposte, throw anybody's manuscript on to the floor? Well, I was goaded, wasn't I? Almost literally. It's not very nice to get a kick in the bottom. Come, come, perhaps you will say, it was only a joke on Uncle Lennox's part. Oh no, is my reply to that. The whole thing took place only under the guise of a joke. There was venom in that kick. I ought to know; it was my bottom.

Well then, you may say, wouldn't it have been more dignified to have left quietly without making any gesture? Oh yes, undoubtedly that is what I would have done if, on my direct route to the french windows, the manuscript hadn't been lying on the drawing-room table just at the height of my passing right hand. And do remember that the whole episode occupied only a few seconds; entry into the drawing-room from a visit to the toilet, Uncle Lennox, Dolly and T. S. Eliot concealed behind the door, unexpected glimpse of Uncle Lennox's long leg shooting out followed by the sensation of a hard kick, picking up the manuscript between my finger and thumb, lifting it up on high, ceremoniously dropping it on to the floor and, without a glance back, sweeping out through the french windows to join my wife Margaret, already making her way up the steep garden path towards the gate. How did I come to realise that it was T. S. Eliot's manuscript? Ah, that is another, and a later, story. In the mean time,

I hope that the reader will forgive this further dive back into the past. In the course of this narrative, the name of Lennox Robinson has cropped up more than once. It is time to gather many things together; to place him in my life.

My uncle and godfather, the late Dr. Lennox Robinson, was the author of *The Whiteheaded Boy* and a great many other plays performed throughout the English-speaking world. I remember his mentioning to me with pride that he had two plays running in London's West End at the same time. He was also the author of dozens of books, though many of them were his plays in book form. His entry in *Who's Who* was very long. But perhaps more importantly, as one of the directors of the very famous Abbey Theatre in Dublin and an editor of *The Oxford Book of Irish Verse*, he was at the centre of the Irish literary movement at the time of W. B. Yeats, Lady Gregory, Sean O'Casey, J. M. Synge, Bernard Shaw, George Moore, Lord Dunsany, and others. It was through him that I met many such.

I met even more through my *Commentary*, the monthy magazine devoted to the arts which for five and a half years I published in Dublin. From its pages emerge to me the enormously vital theatrical, cinematic, artistic, musical and literary life of Dublin in the early forties, much of it centering about the Gate, Gaiety, Olympia and Abbey Theatres, and about the Royal Hibernian Academy and its opponents, when a world war drove the Irish capital in upon its own resources. Yet there were eminent visitors too from England: T. S. Eliot, John Betjeman, Laurence Olivier, Sybil Thorndike, Deborah Kerr, the great pianist Solomon, Joan Hammond the Australian soprano.

As said, I was born in Cork on the south coast of Ireland, was taken out to India when I was a few weeks old, and returned from there with my parents and two sisters when I was nine. No doubt they told me that my Uncle Lennox Robinson, then Manager of the Abbey Theatre, was also my godfather, but I have no memories of him at that time. After putting me into a boarding preparatory school, Castle Park at Dalkey in County Dublin, my parents and two sisters returned to India.

I spent my first school holidays with my maternal grandparents at Ballymoney Rectory (my grandfather was a clergyman in the

111

Protestant Church of Ireland) at Ballineen in County Cork, described by my mother Nora Dorman, her brother Lennox Robinson, and another and older brother Tom Robinson in their book *Three Homes*, published in London by Michael Joseph Ltd. It was a very lonely holiday, passed climbing in the laurels in front of the rectory, made the more lonely by my hearing the voices of the children coming across the fields from Ballineen village some distance away.

My parents came to know of my boredom. Thereafter I was placed in the care of my Uncle Tom Robinson and Aunt Ethel at their flat in Nassau Street in Dublin, with Uncle Lennox Robinson very close by in a flat at number one Clare Street, now the offices of the law firm of Guinan & Sheehan, within walking distance of the Abbey Theatre just across the River Liffey. It was the time of the Irish Civil War. I was often kept awake at night by bursts of machine-gun fire, and even in the daytime there was occasional firing.

But it was a little later that Uncle Lennox really began to make an impression on my child mind. When he did so, it was as the immensely tall, immensely thin, Bohemian, celebrated uncle, who took me on exciting expeditions, introduced me to glamorous theatrical and other famous people, and with whom I was never quite at ease. At the height of his career seemingly with much money to spend, he brought colour and excitement into my life; but Uncle Tom, pipe-smoking, tweedy, soldierly (he had been a captain in the Royal Munster Fusiliers), always living on a shoestring, roused my love and respect. Uncle Tom and Aunt Ethel, with no children of their own, were wonderful foster-parents to me and, later, my sisters also.

But Uncle Lennox did his best for my mother's sake. He adored her. Delicate as a child, he was shut out by his three elder brothers from their games. My mother, sharing his interest in writing, music and painting, was his childhood companion. 'Of course your mother is an angel,' he said to me when I was in my twenties (and so she was). When at the end he was suffering repeated heart attacks, it was with her that he went to stay for a while at the Dorman family home, Raffeen, at that Kinsale in County Cork also mentioned in *Three Homes*.

Sometimes Uncle Lennox would take me out on Sundays from my

prep. school. When winding up my father's and mother's estates at Raffeen, I came across letters from him to my mother in India in which he always gave news of me, referring to me, for her sake of course, as 'The Wonderful Boy'. I remember his taking me to a restaurant in Dalkey. There I would almost silently consume puffy cakes filled with artificial cream, while Uncle Lennox, his thin legs twisted round one another, his string of a form draped round a cup of tea, pointed his long nose at me and watched. I always felt uneasy at accepting yet one more cream puff, knowing that they were costing him all of three pence each, but just as uneasy lest I should not be offered another. It was a difficult situation, rendered yet more difficult by the quizzical smile on his thin-lipped mouth; and by his eyebrows raised in amusement so that his low forehead almost disappeared in wrinkles under a boyish shock of hair. When he saw me back to the school, my heart was bursting with a gratitude that I was too shy to express, and it was with sadness that I saw his long back turn away.

On at least two occasions he took me out to a cottage that he had then acquired at Foxrock near Dublin. I clinging to his back, he rode along very very slowly on a motor-bike, repeatedly calling back to me on the carrier to know if I was all right. Even then, at perhaps ten or eleven years of age, I felt the incongrousness of this utterly unmechanical man, in his floppy eccentric clothes, bow tie, and very broad-brimmed hat, guiding a machine. I don't remember the motor-bike's lasting very long, and he never replaced it with a car. At the Foxrock cottage I met the Abbey Theatre and, later, Hollywood actor Arthur Shiels. I seem to remember there also Dolly Travers, who painted scenery for the Abbey Theatre, and who later became Mrs. Lennox Robinson and, so, my aunt. Everyone was sitting out in the garden, dyeing rushes cut in the grounds and plaiting them into little round mats for the table.

On other occasions I was taken to Dublin, filled with artificial-cream puffs at the Soda Fountain Restaurant in O'Connell Street, and thence to a cinema. By this time I had transferred from my prep. school to a public school, St. Columba's College, five hundred feet up in the Dublin mountains. Being short-sighted, I had been obliged to take to glasses. On one occasion I found myself in the cinema without these, and Uncle Lennox, also short-sighted, lent me his, and himself sat for more than two hours beside me unable properly to see the film. I might have been fifteen at that time.

He also in the holidays took me to see his plays at the Abbey Theatre, to the first-night if possible. Sitting beside me in the stalls, his legs twisted round one another as I've never before or since seen anyone twist their legs, he would laugh with unrestrained enjoyment at his own jokes, although, even on a first night, he must have been seeing the play, rehearsals included, for the twentieth time. Though his enjoyment was unrestrained, his laugh was not. It was partly concealed behind his long bony hand, and emerged as a series of hisses caused by drawing in his breath sharply rather than letting it out. But he would evidently feel the need to explain away his enormous enjoyment of his own comedies, for after a bout of laughter he would turn to me and exclaim how amusing Barry Fitzgerald or F. J. McCormick or Maureen Delany or one of the other players was. This was many years before Barry Fitzgerald left to star in Hollywood films.

Sometimes Uncle Lennox would take me round to the Abbey Theatre Green Room. On one such occasion, meeting Barry Fitzgerald on the way, Uncle Lennox said to him, 'You've only to come on to the stage, and you have them at your feet.' Barry Fitzgerald said nothing, but beamed. Others that I remember in the Green Room were his brother Arthur Shiels, and F. J. McCormick's wife, the actress Eileen Crowe. By this time, I think, Uncle Lennox had risen to being a director of the Abbey Theatre. I also met the fellow director and poet, W. B. Yeats, and Mrs. Yeats.

W. B. Yeats I met on many occasions, if anybody, and particularly a boy, can be said to have 'met' anyone so withdrawn behind, or rather above (for he was tall and stately) a cloud of heaven-only-knew what poetic fancies or philosophical considerations. I watched him one afternoon pacing up and down a lawn with Desmond Fitzgerald, the Minister for Defence, discussing philosophy. Yeats's head, with its leonine mane of hair, was tilted back; his eyes, clouded with abstraction behind their glasses, seemed, as his quiet grave humourless voice sounded on, to fail to notice anything that was happening around him on earth, though they might have been absorbing the aspect of the skies. But above all I was intrigued at that party to watch Ernest Blythe, the Minister for

Finance and later Managing Director of the Abbey Theatre, drive away. His wife and family set off in one car. Then he followed behind them in a second, accompanied by armed detectives.

But to return to the Abbey. Barry Fitzgerald I found very funny (he sometimes stood on the stage without saying a word for moments at a time, convulsing the audience just by the expression on his face), but F. J. McCormick was my hero, whether in comic parts such as the pedlar in Sean O'Casey's *Shadow of a Gunman*, or in high drama such as W. B. Yeats's *Œdipus the King*.

Maureen Delany, my uncle always referred to as 'a wonderful artist', adding in an immediate aside, 'I trained her,' but, though I said nothing, I always found her a very crude performer. However, she was immensely popular as a comedienne with the Abbey Theatre audiences. Although I had at that time, strangely enough, never seen the play, I had always had my Uncle Lennox's name associated with *The Whiteheaded Boy*. When I met Maureen Delany in the Green Room for the first time, she said to my uncle, 'So this is the young nephew that I'm always hearing about!' With an inward shuddering, for I was shy and wanted to be allowed to drop out of the conversation, I felt sure that she was going to add, 'The Whiteheaded Boy!'

She did.

I had made my mark at English and as an actor at my prep. school, and also at English at my public school, where I was awarded a prize in my first term as the best prose writer in competition with boys of up to nineteen. The verse prize was awarded to Nicholas Mansergh, later Dr. Nicholas Mansergh, until recently Master of St. John's College, Cambridge. I followed almost immediately after him as editor of the school magazine. I also won an essay competition open to all the public schools of Great Britain and Ireland. The subject of the essay was, 'Why We Should Be Kind to Animals'. With the prize money I bought a high-powered air-gun and fired at rabbits. I always missed, which I suppose in a way was being kind to them. On account of this (not the airgun, of course) I stood in some favour with the headmaster, or 'Warden' as he was called. Warden the Rev. C. B. Armstrong, though a distinguished classical scholar with his nose buried in Greek and Latin, nevertheless had an eye for English.

One evening I was mysteriously summoned to his study, and

115

thence to his small car. His wife and he sat in front, while I was in an uncovered seat at the back, the chilly Dublin Mountains air blowing round to me as we descended towards the lights winking in the darkness round Dublin Bay. Presently we entered the foyer of the Abbey Theatre, to be greeted by Uncle Lennox. It was the first night of *The Far-Off Hills*, and he had invited all three of us to it.

To my knowledge, it was almost unheard of for a boy to leave the school at night. It was such expeditions, engineered by him with an aggressive charm that no one could gainsay (for all his physical frailness he was very courageous), that made him the Fairy God-father. I was immediately taken with *The Far-off Hills*, and came to the conclusion at the time (perhaps I was wrong) that the two young girls had been modelled on my sisters. The next day my left eye was inflamed. This was set down to the draught that had made its way round to me at the back of the car. For a week I went about the school with half my head in bandages, one-eyed, and unable to wear my glasses. So the fact of my late- night expedition got out, and great was my glory.

I spent part of my holidays at Uncle Lennox's latest home, Sorrento Cottage, at Dalkey on the shores of beautiful Dublin Bay. There my maternal grandmother, since the death of her husband at Ballymoney Rectory in County Cork, acted as his hostess at the parties he gave for Dublin and visiting notables. I remember her pride as she pointed out to me the Minister for This, the Consul-General for That, such and such a writer, artist, actor, musician. At other times I played rolls of Chopin on his pianola, Beethoven's Seventh Symphony, especially the pounding conclusion, over and over again on his cabinet gramophone till everyone's head swam; and felt pride in the pictures by Sir John Lavery, Sir William Orpen, Sean Keating, Harry Clarke and others presented to him by the artists themselves.

There was also the Episode of the Bath. As a healthy normal schoolboy, I naturally regarded washing as an evil to be postponed if it could not be avoided altogether. One morning Uncle Lennox mildly remarked that there were many dark rings round the bath, in which he alleged I had spent two hours the evening before. *Two hours*, he gently emphasised. Very reasonably, I thought, I pointed out to him that this was made necessary by the fact that I hadn't had a bath for a fortnight. He then said that one couldn't, so to speak, save up not-having- baths, the account to be set right from time to time with one super all-embracing gigantic bath. Obviously I found this train of thought confusing, but charitably set it down to something inevitable in the state of being an uncle. However I was an adaptable obliging lad, and thereafter increased the frequency of my bath and diminished the number of rings on it.

I sometimes visited the W. B. Yeats's at their home not far off, where Mrs. Yeats, having somehow heard that I liked meringues, always provided them. I also recall a visit by Sean O'Casey, talking with simple unaffected enthusiasm about some of the pictures he had just seen at the London Tate Gallery, and by his very pretty actress wife. There were many visits by the Abbey Theatre actress, and later producer, Ria Mooney. We also saw a great deal of the artist Dermod O'Brien, President of the Royal Hibernian Academy, and his family.

Warden C. B. Armstrong now advised my parents in India that I should be sent to Oxford, which he told them had the best School of English (the family university was Dublin). Uncle Lennox, as the family's man-of-the-world, what with the publication of his books and the production of his plays in London and New York, was put in charge of the buying of my wardrobe. This he did on a comparatively lavish scale (with my father's money), buying me, for instance, four hats, although I never wore a hat, and a dozen or more white waistcoats to wear with my new 'tails' (bought later), though two or three would have been enough.

When he visited me at Oxford, or later in Paris where I was studying French literature, he pressed a generous number of pound notes into my always impecunious hands. He had written the dialogue for a film set in Ireland, but actually being made at Elstree near London. He was called in, at a large salary, to advise on the general Irishness of the shots as they were taken. 'This is typical Irish countryside,' the English director would exclaim, and when my uncle pointed out that it was not, the director would sweep aside all his objections. So in the end Uncle Lennox, with many wry comments to me, on a visit to Elstree from Oxford, simply lay down on the grass in the sunshine, accepted his large salary, and did nothing. Finally he left to direct one of his own plays in London.

When I came down from Oxford, it was decided that I must be set up as a writer. Uncle Lennox sent me off with a batch of letters

117

of introduction to various celebrated authors, among whom I remember the novelist E. M. Forster in London and the dramatist and Shakespearean producer Granville Barker in Paris. But as I had written nothing, these gentlemen were naturally unable to help me. E. M. Forster, up from his country home to a room he kept in London, gave me a large plate of cherries and one of his articles in 'The New Statesman' (I think) to read. When I admired its construction, he remarked, 'Oh it's like putting together a souffle.'

Granville Barker questioned me closely about the Irish dramatist T. C. Murray's play *Autumn Fire*, which I had never seen but had heard about. In the evening he and his wife took me out in a Rolls-Royce to a film. All the way there he practised his French on the chauffeur. On arrival, he insisted that we should walk one by one from the car to the cinema under an umbrella held up by the chauffeur, although we had nothing more formidable to face than a light drizzle while crossing the width of the pavement.

He invited me to attend a lecture that he was delivering next day at the Sorbonne. His subject was, 'British Dramatists'. I duly turned up with a French friend with whom I had, while promenading up and down the boulevard Saint-Michel, been exchanging lessons in French against lessons in English. Granville Barker devoted much of his lecture to extracts from Sean O'Casey's *The Silver Tassie*, which he read in a high wail that disconcerted me and extracted bursts of applause from the French students. He added, 'If Sean O'Casey knew that I was including him in a talk on *British* dramatists, he'd probably throw a brick at me. However, he has made his home among us, and he is very welcome.' I had been aware, when I was later free-lance writing in that room of mine in Oakley Street in Chelsea, that Sean O'Casey, a Communist, was living just across the Thames in the then Socialist-controlled Borough of Battersea. I had also read the earlier controversy in the Irish press at the time that *The Silver Tassie* was turned down by the Abbey Theatre.

I finally set up in Chelsea, as already described, mainly writing articles for health magazines, drinking first-pressing olive oil bought in bulk direct from a Liverpool importer to increase my weight, sunbathing on my balcony, lifting dumb-bells, and pulling at an expander with rubber strands that sometimes snapped perilously close to my face. One of my uncle's letters of introduction, to a

118

leading London publisher, did bear fruit a year or two later. I received a letter asking if I knew anything about ancient Greece. I rushed round to the Chelsea library, read up in an encylopaedia about Athens, Sparta and Corinth, and replied by return of post that I did. I was then summoned to be a co-translator of a German novel set in the Athens of Alcibiades. In all, over four years, I edited, part re-wrote, or 'ghosted' some half dozen books.

One day the publisher startled me by saying, 'What's this I hear about your uncle's drinking?' Certainly I, an almost non-drinking, non-smoking, expander-pulling, olive-oil drinking health fiend had noticed that Uncle Lennox drank, but so did hundeds of others, and it had never occurred to me that it was a matter for comment. The publisher added, 'He doesn't seem to be doing any work these days.' I replied that he was at that moment writing the script for yet another film, *The Blarney Stone*, directed by Tom Walls in England. 'Yes,' said the publisher with scorn, 'but by the author of *The Whiteheaded Boy!*'

A year or two later when my wife Margaret and I were in Dublin, during the time that I published and edited *Commentary*, my monthly theatrical and art magazine, it was proposed to hold a Book Fair at the Mansion House. Uncle Lennox got me on to the committee, composed of writers, publishers and booksellers. I had been irritated, like many others, by the severity and bigotry of the Irish book censorship at that time. I had campaigned against it in *Commentary*, both directly and by implication, finally being dubbed anti-Catholic and losing my Catholic associate editor, who had pressure put on him to leave.

When I was bringing over to Dublin my Oxford books, running from Chaucer up to about Swinburne, the tea-chest in which they were packed was opened by the Customs. The books were far enough back in time to be passed, all except a paper-backed novel by Louis Bromfield which I had been given by a friend but which I hadn't read. As he confiscated it, the Customs officer said to comfort me, 'Ah, but sure 'tis a queer gloomy kind of a book.' Well, I suppose there was something to be said for trying to keep gloom out of Ireland.

Lectures were to be given daily at the Book Fair by Irish authors. When I saw authors of moment and independence like Sean

O'Faolain and Frank O'Connor being vetoed by the committee, and lesser safer men being put in their place, I at once perceived in this the hand of priestly domination. The burden of the remarks passing about the room (the meetings were held in the premises of the publishers and booksellers James Duffy & Co. Ltd., then situated in Westmoreland Street) was to the effect that Sean O'Faolain and Frank O'Connor had been in collision with the censorship authorities, and that it would be impolitic to invite them to speak. They edited the outspoken and excellent literary review, *The Bell*, already referred to.

A bookseller, I'm pretty sure it was Mr. E. O'Keeffe of the above firm who was honorary secretary to the committee, made the point that as the booksellers were carrying the main financial burden of the venture, they should have a large say in the selection of the authors. This was granted. (In a meeting held after the Book Fair to review events, it was generously agreed by the booksellers and publishers on the committee that it was the author-speakers who had brought in the public and made the Fair a success.)

I have fairly recently corresponded with Sean O'Faolain on the matter of his and Frank O'Connor's exclusion. Of course he could not know what happened in the committee room. He was kind enough to send me a photostat of an appendix to a book by another author on the censorship. The passage is headed, 'Appendix 2 — A Selection of Books Prohibited 1930 — 1946, compiled from the *Register of Prohibited Publications* (as on 31 December 1943) and from the *Irish Oifigiuil*.' The following are included, all not too far removed from the date of the committee meeting concerned: Sean O'Faolain's *Midsummer Night Madness* (banned 22 April 1932) and *Bird Alone* (banned 1 September 1936, but later the subject of a revocation order); and Frank O'Connor's *Dutch Interior* (banned 12 July 1940, but later the subject of a revocation order). However, the eminent status of Sean O'Faolain was recognised by a wiser head than any on the committee when the Minister, Sean Moylan, nominated him Chairman of the Davis Book Week in 1945.

Finally Uncle Lennox, the originator of the idea of the Book Fair, was himself vetoed. I flew at the throats of the committee. Everyone looked very embarrassed. It was tactfully brought home to me by hints that, because of his drinking, he could not be trusted to appear in public without creating some scene. I then remembered the London publisher's words. I withdrew all my objections, but the committee, which was full of his friends, for he had a great capacity for friendship, insisted that he should introduce a speaker and chair a lecture. I couldn't see that this would help very much. It was true that each speaker was being allocated half an hour, but each chairman was being given ten minutes to introduce the speaker, and ten minutes seemed to me almost as good as half an hour for doing any damage, if damage was to be done.

As we emerged from the committee meeting one of the members, I'm pretty sure that it was the secretary Mr. O'Keeffe, approached me. He said words to the effect that we must be guided by the views of eminent and learned churchmen. I replied that I was a writer whose trade was ideas, and that I would in no wise permit my mind to be shackled by that of anyone else whomsoever.

I had been commissioned by Uncle Lennox to bring him the list of speakers and chairmen. I found him sitting alone in the tiny Peacock Theatre which was in the same building as the Abbey Theatre. His pupils of the Abbey Theatre School of Acting had just departed. His mind was thick from drink, and he had difficulty in absorbing what I was telling him. I watched the anger gathering in his leaden eyes as he realised that he had virtually been passed over. He repeated several times, 'Gawd' (a favourite intentional mis-pronunciation of 'God') 'it was I that thought of the whole thing!' He began to vent his wrath on me. This, in view of the circumstances, I didn't feel like stomaching. Regarding his classes for the School of Acting, I was told that he once said, 'I can't take my classes unless I'm drunk,' to which a loyal pupil replied, 'And *I* couldn't be taken unless *I* was drunk.'

The Book Fair was to last four days. With the help of an artist friend Kenneth Hall, my wife Margaret and I, having little money, managed to set up a stall from which to sell our magazine *Commentary*. During one of the committee meetings I had requested permission to do so, saying that I couldn't see any principle that could be urged against it. The members agreed that there was no valid reason to bar it, though all looked their unspoken doubts. I didn't blame them at the time, nor do I now. Who could feel confident about admitting a small periodical then in its infancy?

What kind of a stall might be created for it in comparison with the wellfound stalls of the established booksellers and publishers? In the outcome, with simple materials, Margaret's good taste, and Kenneth Hall's artist's brush, we didn't manage too badly.

On a particular day, while Margaret managed the stall, it was my turn, duly wearing my committee-member badge, to check tickets at one of the doors. Three or four people appeared on their way to the box-office. One of them detached himself, announced that he was Patrick Kavanagh the poet, and that as the Book Fair was for writers he should be allowed to enter without paying. I had at that time vaguely heard of him on a few occasions, I think in connection with some civil action. I was told that he liked to seek publicity. He tried to push past me. Filled with the indignation of a badge-bearer, I belligerantly blocked his way. Two friends seized him, announced that they would buy his ticket, and hauled him off.

When my stint on the door was finished, I wandered round the large hall. Seeing Uncle Lennox, I approached him. I observed that he was talking to Patrick Kavanagh. Also that he was, as had become quite usual, in an aggressive mood. He made some vague reference to my having blocked Patrick Kavanagh's way, contemptuously regarded my badge, and with one finger flicked my tie out of place. Patrick Kavanagh said nothing throughout. Possibly Uncle Lennox had got me on to the committee to guard his interests, and thought that I had failed him. In view of the circumstances, I felt unable to give him the true position. For old times' sake I passed the matter off as agreeably as might be, and departed.

When the time for the lecture arrived, Uncle Lennox rose to his thin six foot plus to introduce the main speaker, the even taller Denis Johnston. In earlier years, when I was free-lancing in Chelsea, I had seen Denis Johnston's *Bride for the Unicorn*, brought over to the London Westminster Theatre by Lord Longford's company. I had sent reports on the reception of the play to some of the Dublin newspapers. His play, *The Moon in the Yellow River*, had been put on by Bernard Shaw at his Malvern Festival. I had also seen his *The Old Lady Says No!*, staged by Hilton Edwards and Micheal MacLiammoir at the Dublin Gaiety Theatre, and had written a long critique of it in *Commentary*. All theatrical Dublin knew the story that Denis Johnston had so entitled his play because Lady Gregory, 'the old lady', Director of the Abbey Theatre, had turned it down. And much of theatrical Dublin believed that the story was false.

Great was my embarrassment when Uncle Lennox began to labour the point. 'The old lady did *not*,' he cried in his high thin voice, hammering on the table with the tops of his long fingers. 'The old lady said, "Yes, yes, yes!"' He proceeded to repeat the statement. When the audience tittered, he began to rate them like children. Laughter broke out. I drew comfort from this, for I thought: They just find him genuinely amusing. This idea was killed when a man sitting immediately in front of me said to his neighbour, 'He's never sober.' I don't know how the scene ended. I heard a kind voice speaking to me, turned to see a well-known Dublin publisher who had been on the committee, and found that I was standing at the far end of the hall with my back turned to the platform. How I got down there I shall never know.

So began to end the bright beginning of Fairy Godfather and Whiteheaded Boy. Some time later I wrote, at the request of Lord Longford, a burlesque of Chekov's *The Three Sisters*, which he had just been staging at the Gate Theatre. My burlesque was acted by a mixed company from Hilton Edwards and Micheal MacLiammoir's Dublin Gate Theatre Company and Lord Longford's Company. Both companies shared the Gate Theatre six months turn and turn about, but Hilton Edwards always insisted to me that *his* company was *the* Gate Theatre Company. Both he and Lord Longford from time to time wrote articles for *Commentary*.

He was equally insistent that, despite the shape of his nose, he was not a Jew. In proof, he averred that he had been a choir boy at, I think, an Anglican church in England (he was English). In further proof, he offered at any time to drop his trousers. I never took him up on this, partly because we were usually walking down O'Connell Street or in St. Stephen's Green. Also, I wasn't much interested; sufficient for me that he was an extremely fine actor and producer. (Throughout this book I have necessarily used the words 'producer' and 'director' indiscriminately, because the theatre people who spoke to me generally did. The words had not then, under the influence of the cinema, settled down to their present precisely differentiated meanings.)

The Chekov burlesque was given three performances in a large marquee in the grounds of Lord and Lady Longford's town house. It was the main item in a garden party held annually to raise funds for the Gate Theatre, and it got good notices in the Dublin papers.

The next day or so, with my wife Margaret and the actor who had directed my play, I made my way out to Dalkey. Margaret and I had been asked to one of Uncle Lennox's parties for Dublin notables in the realms of art, politics and diplomacy. T. S. Eliot had come over to Dublin to give a lecture in the Abbey Theatre, Uncle Lennox was putting him up, and no doubt the party was for him. My grandmother had died, Uncle Lennox had married the artist Dolly Travers, and she of course was hostess on this occasion.

On our arrival, I introduced the actor to Uncle Lennox as 'my producer', with a comic inflexion in my voice, for I didn't want to make too much of my little burlesque. Uncle Lennox first received this in a stony silence. A little later he began to be rude to me in a childish way in front of some journalists. For old times' sake I persisted in replying pleasantly, but finally was driven to saying, 'Oh, don't be absurd!' Uncle Lennox departed. I smiled apologetically at the journalists, the journalists smiled back, and melted away.

Why oh why did he do it? Because he was jealous of the notices in the Dublin papers? My one burlesque, when he had a whole string of plays to his name? Yet he might have seen it as the beginning of a challenge on his very own ground. But he was so generous in helping playwrights, and had given me most useful criticism on an earlier play of mine dealing with the life of Van Gogh, *Sunflowers in Arles*. I suspect that he bought my *Commentary* off the stalls of the Dublin newsagents. He showed no particular spleen when, later, my novel set among Donegal scenes and characters, *Brigid and the Mountain*, was published by Peter Davies in London and Recommended by the Book Society.

Was it just the bad temper of a man whose mind and body are irritated by drink? A leading actor of Lord Longford's Company, Blake Gifford, who had played the principal role in my burlesque and who was at St. Columba's College some time before me, had refused to come to the party with Margaret and me, saying, 'Your uncle terrifies me.' Was it the outcome of a love-hate relationship, for Uncle Lennox had asked me out to his house on several occasions, yet been unpleasant to me when I arrived? The inability on his part to accept the sadness that comes to many a parent or foster-parent, when their once hero-worshipping charge grows a stubborn personality of his own and now can no longer be managed and influenced? The resentment and contempt so often felt by the drinker for the sobersides, because of the uneasy unacknowledged feeling that his habit may be robbing him of a health that the other is preserving?

When the time came to leave, I entered the drawing-room to say goodbye. All the other visiting guests had already gone. I felt a hard kick in my stern. I looked round to see that it had been delivered by Uncle Lennox. Dolly, T. S. Eliot and he had hidden behind the drawing-room door. Knowing him, I realised that he had organised the business under the guise of a joke, but the strength of that kick also told me that there was no laughter in his heart. Without looking back again, I walked out of the room by some french windows that gave on to the lawn.

As I passed a small table, I saw a typescript lying on it. Supposing it to be my uncle's, I picked it up and dropped it on to the floor, also under the guise of a joke. As I made my way up the garden, I heard Dolly's voice raised in protest calling, 'Sean! Sean!' Suddenly I realised what that typescript, a very thick one, was. It was nice, courteous T. S. Eliot's lecture for the Abbey Theatre.

I joined Margaret, who had been wandering on ahead of me towards the gate. I made up my mind that it was useless trying to mix oil and water. I must keep away from the Fairy Godfather in future, before all the magic had fled. I owed him much. Because I owed him much, I had put up with much. But it was achieving nothing. There was plainly going to be no end to it. Had our natures been similar, something might have been managed — possibly. Dolly, though herself quite a heavy 'social drinker', as the phrase goes, finally refused to accompany him on his lecture tours in the United States, or even to attend his first nights at the Abbey Theatre. 'I'm not going to sit there,' she once said to me, 'wondering if he's going to fall flat on the stage when taking a curtain call.'

But Uncle Lennox's and my natures were sharply different, in more ways than one. I believed in live and let live, to such a degree that

125

it never occurred to me, left to myself, to question his drinking. I was wholly astonished when the London publisher had done so. When Margaret and I, existing on the usual shoestring associated with young married couples pursuing the arts, on one occasion invited Dolly and Uncle Lennox to supper at our flat in the Dublin suburb of Clontarf, our chief concern lay in how to raise the money to buy Uncle Lennox a bottle of whisky. But a little later, when Uncle Lennox entertained the actor Tom Purefoy and myself to lunch at the Dublin Gresham Hotel, things took an opposite turn. I ordered a salad. Uncle Lennox looked me up and down contemptuously and remarked with an equally contemptuous inflexion, 'He's thinking of his figure.' What's sauce for the goose is sauce for the gander! If those who drink have a right to their place in the sun, so have those who pursue health.

There will be some who will say, from the safety and comfort of a deep and distant armchair, that alcoholism is a disease and that Uncle Lennox should have been sustained and endured. I wonder, if they had arisen and descended into the arena, how notable their own performance would have been. Uncle Lennox had the help of a clergyman who was also a psychiatrist. The outcome was failure. After I had left to work in England, I heard that Dublin University had conferred upon him a Doctorate of Literature. I wrote him my congratulations. He replied warmly. A little later, at no great age, he was dead. He was accorded a national funeral, and buried at St. Patrick's Cathedral.

But, as far as this book is concerned, his Presence does not end there . . .

AFTERTHOUGHT

It seems, for all Uncle Lennox's vehemence to the contrary, that Denis Johnston himself more than half believed that the 'Old Lady' was indeed Lady Gregory, and that her 'No' was indeed a no to his play. When he received it back from the Abbey Theatre, the words 'the Old Lady says no' were written on a sheet of paper attached to the front of it. The play was not produced at the Abbey, though the management partly subsidised its performance at the little Peacock Theatre in the same building. Lady Gregory expressed her dislike of it to Denis Johnston, when she met him in a hotel in Harcourt Street. She never invited him to her home in the west of Ireland, where so many were welcomed.

Chapter Ten
Hilton Edwards & Micheal MacLiammoir

While at Castle Park Preparatory School, at St. Columba's College, and at Worcester College Oxford, I had of course met many people of the theatre through Lennox Robinson. One such occasion was when, during the first interval of a play at a London Theatre (I had come up to town from Oxford), a man greeted my uncle effusively. I wondered why I was not introduced. As the man departed, Uncle Lennox put up his long bony hand and murmured from behind it, 'Gawd, I don't know who he is!' Again in the second interval the man approached, conversed, and I could not be introduced. As in all well made dramas, the situation was screwed up to a new height of tension when the man nailed us in the foyer at the end of the performance and invited us both to a club. Uncle Lennox felt unable to refuse; plainly he was being regarded as a very close friend.

Fortunately the man had invited a few other guests. Uncle Lennox was able to discover from one of them that our host was the eminent dramatist and critic, Ashley Dukes. His brilliance, on the evidence of that evening at least, appeared to channel itself exclusively down his pen. We found him dull, without personality. I wasn't surprised that Uncle Lennox had failed to remember him. He seemed to be one of those people designed by nature to pass unnoticed, camouflaged in a grey nothingness that merged with city smog and mud-splashed buses.

Of course this impression, founded on a single encounter, might have been quite unjust. Indeed could it be true of Ashley Dukes, author of *The Man With a Load of Mischief* in which Fay Compton scored so resounding a success; of the considerably modified English version of the Spanish play *La Celestina*, which provided Sybil Thorndike with so many humorous opportunities; the dramatic critic of *The Illustrated Evening News* and of *The Star*; the English editor of the American *Theatre Arts Monthly*; the proprietor of the small but distinguished Mercury Theatre where not only so many of his adaptations of French and German plays were performed, but where his wife Marie Rambert staged those ballets which contributed so greatly to the development of the art in Britain? Perhaps, like many writers, he preferred to sit quietly and watch the world rather than be watched by it.

Included in the small party was the Chinese author of the then highly successful play, *Lady Precious Stream*. While he discussed theatre with my uncle and a middle-aged actress, his slant-eyed tiny wife, with features like a doll, and dressed in a high-collared royal-blue gown with a dragon embroidered in gold thread winding its way up her petite figure, sat never uttering a word. The contrast between her dainty oriental self-effacement, and the relatively large-featured, European-emancipated, voluable actress, fascinated me. Later the actress said to me, 'I noticed you couldn't take your eyes off her.' 'No,' I replied. 'I kept wanting to pick her up between my finger and thumb and put her on a mantlepiece.'

But by far the greater number of my theatrical acquaintances came to me, not through my uncle, but through my monthly periodical *Commentary*. First of them, apart from Lord and Lady Longford, and their director John Izon, and certain members of their theatre company, was the director and actor Hilton Edwards. This was because he was one of the Vice-Presidents of Margaret's Picture Hire Club.

Hilton Edwards had invited me to attend any of his rehearsals that I cared to. At this time they took place in a large mostly unfurnished room, I forget where. I lounged in an armchair, watching with half an eye, listening with half an ear, and writing. At a much later time a member of his company said to me, 'We always used to wonder what you were writing.' I had no idea that I was being particularly noticed. Thinking back now, it may have been a little unnerving for the cast to feel that there and then their every move was perhaps being noted down by a journalist who owned the only theatre magazine in Dublin. Actually, I had merely being writing a book that had nothing whatever to do with the rehearsal.

Hilton Edwards licked his actors into shape not only by verbal exhortation, but also on occasion by seizing one or other of them by the arm and dragging him into position. They took this in good part, because they knew that the outcome was always a stage presentation at a very high level. They also in effect were getting a free lesson in their trade at the hands of an exceedingly fine actor.

Hilton Edwards, an Englishman, was introduced in London to the Irish actor-manager, Anew MacMaster. Anew MacMaster was looking for a leading man at short notice. So over to Ireland, where he was to make so great an impact, Hilton Edwards went, playing such roles as Macduff, and The King in *Hamlet*. Anew MacMaster, being an actor-manager with a personal following, filled the top roles himself. When on one occasion he hired the Abbey Theatre to put on a performance of *Othello*, he entrusted the part of Iago to Hilton Edwards. The latter was severely handled by the critics for rendering the character at the speed that he did. He always maintained to me that American speed was twice as fast as English, and English speed was twice as fast as Irish.

One of the last plays in which he appeared before crossing to Ireland was a Jewish drama, *Dybukk*, at the London Royalty Theatre. Jean Forbes Robertson was in the cast. During Hilton Edwards' first season with Anew MacMaster, he met Micheal MacLiammoir. With Micheal MacLiammoir he set up what was to become a vivid and creative partnership, bringing back vitality into the dramatic life of Dublin. Dublin had, off and on, been a notable centre of theatre down the centuries. But the once illustrious Abbey Theatre, after the deaths of Lady Gregory, Synge and W. B. Yeats, the self-imposed exile to England of Sean O'Casey, and Lennox Robinson progressively ceasing to be a directing force, was to languish under a management lacking theatrical verve and instinct.

Hilton Edwards and Micheal MacLiammoir decided to set up their own theatre. Peter Godfrey, who had been in the cast of the Jewish *Dybukk* at the Royalty in London, and who had initiated his Gate Theatre there, suggested that they should make their new theatre into an Irish 'Gate'. The idea was that they should be of benefit to one another. He was to act for them as a clearing house for interesting

Continental plays, and they in their turn were to send him material. But circumstances in England and Ireland were too different. 'I didn't then realise,' said Hilton Edwards to me, 'that the distance that separated us was much greater than the geographical one. We got pulled apart. He asked me only to safeguard and keep to ourselves the name of "Gate Theatre". The manner in which I have failed to do so is now well known.'

When, on meeting Lord Longford a little later, I suggested that this blade had been thrust at him, his riposte was energetic. 'Hilton Edwards, Micheal MacLiammoir and I used to run the theatre together. I was at least as much responsible for policy as they were. I myself chose, with their approval, many of their most successful plays. This is quite apart from any financiel assistance I gave. It's well known that I bore the entire burden of loss, which was extremely heavy. Eventually we disagreed so fundamentally on questions of administration that a break became inevitable. The arrangement then come to was a fifty-fifty one, both sides having the use of the theatre, if they required it, for half the year. As a matter of fact, for the last three years' (Lord Longford was speaking to me in the April of 1944) 'Mr Edwards and Mr MacLiammoir have hardly played in the Gate at all.'

The first time that I ever really came across Micheal MacLiammoir (even then I spoke not a single word to him) was at one of Hilton Edwards' rehearsals. Before that he had filtered through to me only via a variety of hushed rumours. These had built up in my mind a vague impression of a handsome, debonair and scandalous fellow strolling across St Stephen's Green in daringly individual clothes, hat and walking-cane a-swagger, fingers be-ringed, wearing make-up. He spoke French and Irish fluently, so it was said. The snippets of information died away into significant murmurs. A boulevardier who spoke French and Irish fluently and wore rings and make-up! Whatever next! Nelson's Column in O'Connell Street (only much later was it blown up by nationalists) was observed to sway.

During the rehearsal Hilton Edwards, in his capacity as director, at one point had occasion to tell Micheal MacLiammoir not merely what to do, but why. This last entailed his expounding to him in a word or two the psychology of the character that he was portraying.

'I know all that,' snapped Micheal MacLiammoir.

In the depths of my chair, I paused from my writing. Here was a clash of the Titans! The other actors were but hired hands, but this was partner against partner. What would happen? In the distance rolled Wagnerian thunder. Lightning flickered over Valhalla. Heroes and gods alike were alerted.

Hilton Edwards' face was concerned.

The testiness in Micheal MacLiammoir's died. 'I didn't mean that I knew what action I should take on the stage. I promise you I didn't mean that.'

'Oh,' said Hilton Edwards, accepting the apology.

Well, that was fair enough. Micheal MacLiammoir was not only a highly intelligent actor, but a dramatist of no mean insight, the reader of plays to his partner. Early every summer, as soon as they had finished their spring season, the question would be asked, 'What shall we do next autumn?' The hundreds of new plays were read aloud, usually by Micheal, with Hilton Edwards attentively puffing his pipe. MacLiammoir's pride as a writer of plays, and one of the two selectors of the piece being rehearsed, had been touched on the raw by the implication that he needed to have his part explained to him. On the other hand he was too good a man of the theatre to suppose that, involved as he was in the action, he could see the proportions of the stage picture, the unity of the piece, the effect of his own performance, with the same clarity as the man out in front seated in the detached involvement of the director's chair.

Sybil Thorndike remarked to me when on a visit to Dublin at a later date, 'There was always some sort of a stage director, a skipper. You get more unity with a producer. A lot of actors owe everything to the producer. A producer was merely a director before; now he teaches them how to act.' She added after thought, 'But I think that the thing can be overdone. A producer's ideal function is to keep in check and in balance a lot of vital, violently excitable, individuals, and not to be just a schoolmaster.'

In order to get news of their forthcoming productions for my magazine *Commentary*, from time to time I visited Hilton Edwards at their flat. Mostly I conversed with him in their living-room, but on one occasion I went into an adjoining office. 'It's absurd,' said Edwards, pointing at some filing cabinets. 'We're supposed to be actors, but it's nine tenths office work and one tenth acting.'

On one of these occasions, I was sitting in the living-room making notes of what Hilton was saying on some sheets of paper on my lap. Micheal MacLiammoir, garbed in a dressing-gown, appeared at a doorway. Hilton Edwards began to rate him. 'You're a disgrace, coming in like that. Just look at you! Bits of stale make-up all over your face! Just go and wash yourself!' Embarrassed, I glanced at MacLiammoir to see how he was taking it. He was standing with a half smile on his face, loving it all. Finally, in obedience to Edwards' commands, he withdrew unhurriedly.

If Micheal painted himself, he painted also scenery for the Gate Theatre, at least initially. His work was most distinctive. It was his decor, together with Hilton's determination to mount his productions at a high standard of lighting, costuming and wigs, that gave the Gate Theatre its undoubted excitement and individuality. The building may have been shabby externally but, from the moment one entered the foyer with its posters, all was glamour. The plain auditorium was lambent with the half-light of theatrical occasion.

Once upon a time the then equally shabby building of the Abbey Theatre, formerly the city morgue, with its black and gold curtain rising on the sounding of a gong; Dr. Larchet in the orchestra pit conducting from the piano his otherwise string ensemble in classical music; Dermod O'Brien and the politician Bryan Cooper on a first night filling the front rows with their evening-gowned and dinner-jacketed guests; Uncle Lennox, Dolly and I joining them; the tall burly lion-locked W. B. Yeats, his spectacles attached by a length of black ribbon to his person, haunting the foyer; a Synge or Sean O'Casey play upon the stage sustained by the great acting of F. J. McCormick, of Barry Fitzgerald — once the Abbey Theatre was lit by the same light, or so it seemed to my youthful eyes. But now no more. Then there were giants in the land. Now, for the most part, there were ghosts only.

On the birth of our eldest child Paul, Margaret and I, having discovered that no self-respecting landlord or landlady would accept a baby into their premises (they appeared to be united in a passionate resolve to extinguish the human species), had at length discovered a haven a little way out of Dublin in a cottage on a farm at Baily on Howth peninsula. It often amused me, as I reclined in a haystack clad only in trunks sunbathing and typing a letter, to reflect how little the recipient would guess where the official-looking missive, with its printed central-Dublin address, had been produced. The address was that of the printers, The Sackville Press, just off the end of O'Connell Street.

The main room of the cottage was the flag-stoned kitchen with its iron range. Off one end of it opened a small bedroom, and off the other, a smaller. There was a minute scullery, and a bathroom not much bigger. We had a lot of books, a lot of pictures, and no furniture. Our table was given to us by one of Margaret's artists, a French girl called Rondel. Its top was cut out of plywood, and rested uncertainly on the summits of four round legs constructed of layers of cardboard. Rondel, together with producing easel pictures for Picture Hire, also designed fabrics. The bales of cloth were wound on to these cardboard centres. Somewhere we found a bed, and Paul had his cot. Two or three chairs also apparently materialised, for we certainly sat at the table. There I cut out and pasted into place pictures and strips of text on galley proofs to form the make-up of *Commentary*. Little Paul, when he became old enough to do so, sat at my elbow industriously scribbling on pieces of paper and pasting them together. 'Daddy,' he would say, 'I'm doing my "Commissy".' But he wasn't destined to join me in editorship. Now that he has become a very large Paul with a family of his own, he has also become a very successful businessman.

Two of our neighbours were Professor Baily Butler and Anew McMaster. During the First World War, Professor Baily Butler told me, he had been a doctor in the British army. He was now, as I understood, Professor of Archaeology at University College, Dublin. He showed me over his house and grounds. The house he had built himself, including the slating, electrical wiring, and plumbing, assisted only by unskilled labour. On the roof he had installed a great metal hood, painted white on the inside and brilliantly lighted internally. This attracted insects which, on flying under the hood, were overcome by the vapour ascending from camphor and fell into the receptacle. These specimens he was trapping on behalf of a colleague in the college department of entomology.

Out in the grounds, he had installed not only a sundial but also a moondial. He had nurtured a tennis court whose surface, he assured me, was the equal of that of the centre court at Wimbledon.

On two sides of it, hedges ran away into the distance without giving the impression of getting any narrower. He had exactly countered the effect of perspective by increasing gradually the width of the hedge. What were apparently the remains of a Greek temple, he had constructed out of fragments of columns bought when the old Customs House in Dublin was being demolished. The foundation stone of the temple had been laid by his wife with a gold and silver trowel, made of course by himself. The 'gold' took the form of a sovereign implanted in the silver shaft. Before he was allowed to do this, he had to obtain the permission of the Bank of Ireland.

A few days later I was seated in Anew McMaster's living-room, discussing his future theatrical plans. He was a very large man. I had seen him, his chest bared, dominating the centre of the stage as a highly imposing 'Othello'. He was also a very nervous man. The Second World War was at its height, and his conversation was quite as much about what he would do and say if Hitler's Nazis suddenly were to walk into his house, as it was about his forthcoming productions. I don't think that he actually expected Adolph Hitler himself. But Doctor Goebbels, the Minister for Propaganda, perhaps . . .

Mrs Anew McMaster, in contrast to her husband a small person, I met too. She appeared to be devoted to him and to his career, and very proud of his stage presence. I had been told that she was Micheal MacLiammoir's sister. Suddenly Micheal MacLiammoir himself appeared in the doorway. Throwing his arms wide apart and marching into the room in the best manner of a stage entrance, in ringing tones he greeted Anew McMaster with the dramatic tidings, 'I've reached the change of life.' Anew McMaster advanced, embraced him, and with all the charm of a kinsman replied, 'You have long passed it.'

I continued to sit by the fire and regard Micheal MacLiammoir curiously. There was something about his walk . . . It wasn't quite a man's, and yet it wasn't a woman's. Then — I got it. It was exactly like the walk of an actress playing the Principal Boy in a pantomime. It was a stage walk. And his voice was a stage voice. I don't mean that he put it on; I'm sure that he had no other. But it was a cultivated measured voice. Deep, resonant and rounded, it appeared not only to be projected from his vocal apparatus, but to have had its total origins there. It didn't seem to grow out of his entire being. He was, it seemed, a sensitive man living behind a protective front.

Hilton Edwards's, on the other hand, when he strode along beside me voluably unburdening his rich mind, poured out in an unselfconscious naturalness. He seemed to have grown up in the hurly-burly of life, perhaps a rough Cockney life. He told me of one occasion when the Dublin-slum-raised Sean O'Casey gave him the rough edge of his tongue in some negotiations over an O'Casey play. Hilton Edwards returned as good as he got. As he expressed it to me, 'I too was born with my hands on my hips.'

Chapter Eleven
Sybil Thorndike W B Yeats

Anew McMaster was somewhat older than Hilton Edwards and Micheal MacLiammoir. To him there never seemed to have been a time when he didn't take it for granted that he would go on to the stage. He had seen all the great actors of the generation before him: Beerbohm Tree, Ellen Terry, Sarah Bernhardt, Mrs Patrick Campbell, Fred Terry, Marie Tempest, Juia Neilson. Anew McMaster told me that Julia Neilson and her husband Fred Terry appeared in the original production of *The Scarlet Pimpernel*, and he with them.

I myself saw him acting with Mrs Patrick Campbell, whom he had brought over to Dublin on her last visit there. It was at the Abbey Theatre. At the beginning of the week I saw them in Shakespeare's *Macbeth*, and at the end in Ibsen's *Ghosts*. On both occasions I was in the company of Uncle Lennox. Lennox Robinson was watching with admiration Mrs Patrick Campbell — as a woman. 'The line of her neck!' he breathed with a smile, drawing it with his finger in the air. I glanced at the whiteness, emphasised by the low neckline of the black dress, of the back of her (to me) elderly neck, poked slightly forward. In the arrogance of youth, I much preferred the sprightly carriage of some pert bobby-soxer.

In 1943 Hilton Edwards and Micheal MacLiammoir presented Sybil Thorndike to Dublin during one of their seasons at the large Gaiety Theatre. While over from England, she was also able to visit Sir Lewis Casson's and her son Christopher Casson, who was playing at the Gate Theatre in Lord Longford's company. The first play was a comedy, Shaw's *Captain Brassbound's Conversion*. The second was a tragedy, Isben's *Ghosts*. Not only were these plays chosen as two that required an exceptional personality to bring them to their full life, but also because they were parts which she knew already (if not made her own). The duration of her war-time permit left little time for rehearsals.

Before coming over to Dublin, she, with her husband Lewis Casson, in 1940 had undergone weeks of anxiety over their eldest son, John Casson, reported missing and believed killed in action. Later it was discovered that he had been taken prisoner by the Germans. Lewis Casson persuaded Guthrie, who was running the London Old Vic Theatre (closed by the war), to allow him to take the company out of the bombing and westward to Wales. As their production, Casson chose Shakespeare's *Macbeth*. 'I know the Welsh people,' he said. 'I'm Welsh myself. They like a tragedy.' As the bombing of London grew worse, Guthrie gave the order, 'Leave Paddington station at noon if Paddington station is still there at noon.' After the Welsh touring was finally over in 1942, Sybil Thorndike, with Henry Ainley, Edith Evans and Leslie Howard, led a vast company in an *Anthology in Praise of Britain*, staged in front of St Paul's Cathedral. Later this was re-enacted amidst the ruins of Coventry Cathedral.

One of my conversations with Sybil Thorndike took place racing towards the Gaiety Theatre. She had been seeing her son Christopher Casson, and was late for a rehearsal. Racing down Dublin pavements beside actors! There was Hilton Edwards . . . The only difference between Hilton Edwards and Sybil Thorndike, in this respect, was that she walked and talked even faster, at least when late for a rehearsal. Her sturdy tweed-jacketed figure kept half a stride ahead of me.

I asked her what attributes an actor should have.

'Personality and instinct and, if he's to become something more than a good actor, something burning to express. There must be terrific work always. I'm good on work and something to express; I had something to say and terrific energy.'

I found myself, as I pounded along after her, able to accept her word for this last. 'What part of your early training did you find most useful?'

'I think Shakespeare repertory. By "repertory" I mean real repertory, not the modern week by week version which passes for repertory. This latter is a wicked imposition, detrimental to any actor. It's more than hard work; it's ridiculous. A real repertory is having a repertoire of ten or eleven plays. These are performed, as they do on the Continent, turn about for two days each. The modern idea of repertory is not repertory at all. It's the equivalent of the old-fashioned stock company.'

'Your first roles?'

'I started acting when I was four. All the amateur work I did was very valuable. My professional work began when I was eighteen. I played all the Shakespearean parts, male and female, that were suitable and lots that were not. After I had played all the women's parts that were not starred, I finally got to the stars.'

'What are your preferences among playwrights?'

'Shaw, Shakespeare, Ibsen, the Greeks. Of the quite moderns, Van Druten, Maugham.'

'Whom do you regard as the most accomplished among present actors and actresses?'

'I think Laurence Olivier is the most vital. I think also of John Gielgud. Edith Evans is a great actress, in my opinion. She is *great*. I don't think we have any men of her stature.'

I found it interesting to get a younger actress's view of Sybil thorndike. That actress was Meriel Moore. She formed, with Coralie Carmichael and Betty Chancellor, the highly accomplished feminine triumvirate who added so much further strength and lustre to Hilton Edwards' and Micheal MacLiammoir's company. Her first parts, obtained through my Uncle Lennox, were at the Abbey Theatre. Later she joined Edwards-MacLiammoir, and later again played in Lennox Robinson's *Is Life Worth Living* (*Drama at Inish* was its title at its Abbey Theatre premiere) at the Ambassadors Theatre in London. There it ran for four months. She was with Edwards-MacLiammoir during Sybil Thorndike's visit and acted with her.

'Sybil Thorndike's work,' she said to me, 'represents my ultimate ideal in acting — flawless technique accompanied by great feeling and imagination, complete truth in conception and representation, a beautiful voice fully developed and perfectly used. Like most great artists, she works all the time. When she's not actually rehearsing or playing, she learns parts or poems to keep her memory in training. Or she reads aloud to herself and does voice exercises. Our company as a rule rehearses all afternoon, and of course we play at night.

Sybil Thorndike asked for morning rehearsals in addition. So we worked all day as well as at night. Personally, I would cheerfully have abandoned sleep and worked through the night as well.'

'And the performance itself?'

'It's obvious to anyone how fine are her great dramatic moments, her big scenes. But I was even more enthralled by little simple things so perfectly done, ordinary theatrical 'business' made interesting and alive: using a handkerchief, opening a door, sewing, moving a book. An actor in the company remarked that you could leave her alone on the stage for half an hour with nothing to do but darn a stocking, and she would hold the audience perfectly for the whole thirty minutes.

'As an example of what I mean, in act one of *Ghosts* she has a rather long scene during which she hardly speaks. To occupy herself, she winds a skein of wool into a ball. She has played Mrs Alving many times and presumably rehearsed it a great deal. Therefore she must have wound that skein hundreds of times. Yet it has never become mechanical or stagy. Nor does it for an instant distract attention from the dialogue; it is used with consummate skill to show her reactions to the scene. The slightest hesitation in the winding, a quick shake of the skein, a pause as she glances up at the speaker; it is perfection.

'There are many more moments in her beautiful performance of Mrs Alving. There are domestic scenes which she plays with such quite strength, such true inner force and feeling, and with such vocal beauty, that they moved me to almost more admiration than the big dramatic moments in the last act.'

'Anew McMaster spoke of her as being, in private, a charming person.'

'Yes indeed. The final thing which makes working with her such a pleasure is Sybil Thorndike herself. Understanding, amusing, thoughtful and kind, helpful whether one brings her one's domestic or one's theatrical troubles. It's quite impossible to treat her as Dame Sybil Thorndike, with the respect due to her position. She just waves it aside and makes one laugh. She remarked one day in the theatre, apropos some conversation about the future, "It makes me so furious that my life must come to an end." I can't believe that it ever will. She is the very embodiment of life.'

I said that Anew McMaster was a very large and a very nervous man. (He was also totally unaffected and honest.) I mentioned his preoccupation with the possibility that, in neutral Ireland, a squad of Hitler's storm-troopers might at any moment erupt into his living-room. A second occasion when I noticed his nervousness was at the Olympia, a large theatre like the Gaiety. The play was Jean Giraudoux's *Amphitryon 38*.

In accord with his imposing physique, Anew McMaster was playing the role of Jupiter. As was only proper, Shelah Richards the director had arranged for Jupiter to descend out of the heavens. During a dress rehearsal two ropes, with a bar arranged across their ends like the seat of a swing, were lowered from the flies. A similar contraption was lowered at the other side of the stage. This latter was for Dennis Barry, a small slight man playing the part of Mercury. Each actor stepped on to his respective bar and took hold of his respective pair of ropes.

Both began to be hauled up towards the lofty proscenium arch. Dennis Barry sustained the ever increasing distance above the stage with the utmost calm, and Anew McMaster in the utmost terror. The contrast between the small and slender Mercury balancing unperturbed upon his perch, and the mighty Jupiter in his majestic robes, having let go one of his ropes, clinging in panic with both hands and bowed head to the other, filled me (how very foolishly, I fully appreciated only later) with impatience.

Recently I took a trip on the vertical 'Giant Wheel' at a fair. At the summit of its orbit I discovered that the slightest movement set up a to-and-fro rocking of my seat, threatening to plunge me into the crowd far below. Now I began to understand something of Anew McMaster's predicament. My seat at least was broad, and firm in the crosswise direction, whereas his narrow foothold was unstable in every direction. His size certainly gave him no advantage over the slender Mercury; he would fall with the same velocity and, being possessed of the greater mass, hit the stage a great deal harder. Shelah Richards had to abandon the project.

When, on a later occasion, I put to Laurence Olivier a distinction that Denis Barry had once made to me between an actor's art and an actor's craft, his reply was, 'I don't precisely know what he means. "Art" and "artist" are two very wide terms. I have heard the distinction drawn that such and such a man was a great artist, while such and such another was a great actor. By this, I take it, is meant that the first man was a great personality who always appeared superbly as himself, while the other had the ability to conceal himself behind, and to create, a great variety of characterisations. Thus Marie Tempest might be styled a great artist but a poor actress. When she made no effort to appear as other then herself she was superb, but when she attempted a characterisation she was disappointing.'

After thought, Laurence Olivier added, 'I myself confess to a liking for that kind of acting in which you change from part to part, so that a member of the audience, not possessing a program, wouldn't know who you were. There are restrictions of course. You can alter your appearance, your gestures and your voice. But you couldn't alter your personality to any great extent, not much more than a great painter could alter his style from picture to picture. Personality is the man, the soul, you.'

My own interpretation of what Dennis Barry had in mind would be different. I would think that a great virtuoso like, say, Liszt, highly conscious of the gymnastics, beyond the compass of most other good pianists, which his fingers were accomplishing during the playing of one of his most difficult passages, was on such occasions paramountly concerned with his craft, the mechanics of his trade, the skill and the physical ability that he had acquired. But when I met the great and world-famous Solomon on a visit to Dublin, and watched his playing, I felt that his fingers were not fingers at all but an extension of his mind, their hard- won skill no longer thought of but bent totally to the task of interpreting Bliss or Mozart or Tchaikovsky.

The same distinction was surely being made by implication in Meriel Moore's already quoted remark about the playing of Sybil Thorndike. 'Her work represents to me the ultimate ideal in acting: flawless technique accompanied by great feeling and imagination; complete truth in conception and representation.' Perhaps Dennis Barry's point was that Hilton Edwards' flawless technique wasn't always sufficiently married to, sufficiently warmed by, inner feeling, as was Solomon's, as was Sybil Thorndike's — indeed, as was Laurence Olivier's.

Ria Mooney and Shelah Richards I always associate with my pre-married days at Sorrento Cottage. Their names were among those most frequently on the lips of my Uncle Lennox Robinson and Aunt Dolly. Indeed Ria Mooney visited quite often. When she did so, her dark prettiness invariably fluttered my twenty-year-old heart.

I mentioned to her that Sean O'Casey and his wife had been to tea the day before.

She laughed. 'His wife's very pretty but she's a very poor actress. Oh, she's *very* pretty. She rather set her cap at the up and coming dramatist.'

A little later I attended a very large evening dinner party held at the Gresham Hotel. It was by way of giving a send-off to the Abbey Theatre first company, due shortly to leave for one of their American tours. W. B. Yeats presided at the head of the table made up of many tables placed end to end and stretching the length of the room. Towards the conclusion of the meal everybody began to pass round their menus to have them autographed; there were many distinguished people present.

As the menus reached me, they contained in the list of signatures a name that I recognised as that of a Scots lady with a buxom five-foot-eleven (I would guess) Junoesque snowy-skinned much-made-up daughter whom she was grooming for presentation, it was said, at the court of St James. Uncle Lennox had earlier introduced me to mother and daughter and dragooned me into dancing with the latter. There was dancing in the ballroom where, a year or two earlier, I had had my encounter with the Paul Jones. I escaped from the daughter as soon as might be (it was to the petite and the slender that I was then drawn). This was no mean task, for she was hughly amorous, plainly towards all men.

The Scotswoman had signed her name (I invent a fictitious one on the same model) 'Agnes MacMackintosh of Orkney'. I immediately signed my own as 'Dorman of Oxford and Hell'. Bovine humour? Certainly. But I was still very young and had wined and dined. I passed on the menu to Uncle Tom. At this period Uncle Lennox had got him the job of secretary in the office of the Abbey

Theatre. Uncle Tom had also wined and dined. With an impish half-smile under his dark moustache, I saw him sign the menu 'The Great Mor of Glencullen'. (Penniless as ever, he shortly afterwards had to move from his small farm at Glencullen to a smaller at Ballycorus.) Other people took up the idea. More and more fictitious names appeared as people recycled their menus in the hope of collecting further signatures. I glanced up the table at Yeats; how, as president of the function, was he reacting to all this? He gave no sign. He merely continued, as the menus reached him, methodically to write his usual signature.

To many the greatest poet of the twentieth century, he could be very down-to-earth. When an international motor-racing handicap Grand Prix was held in the Phoenix Park, I went along with Uncle Lennox, Dolly, and Mr and Mrs Yeats. (It always gave me a start when Mrs Yeats addressed her tall, stately, distinguished-looking, grave, and often other-worldly husband as 'Willie'. Truly a prophet is cut down to size in the bed-chamber!) All holders of seats in the grandstand, ourselves among them, were presented with scoring-sheets on which appeared the names of the cars, their numbers, drivers and handicap times.

There were also spaces in which to record the circuits completed by the six litre, and supercharged four and a half litre, Bentleys; the huge seven litre Mercedes-Benz with their outside exhaust-pipes running along the sides of their bodies, the Bugattis, the Lagondas, the Aston-Martins, the Fraser-Nashes, the three cream-coloured Talbots sweeting haughtily round in perfect formation with no intention of winning but merely of demonstrating their reliability and their looks, the seven-horse-power 'Baby' Austins, each bearing an enormous driver and mechanic, the latter having to sit partially sideways in the small cockpit with his arm round the driver's back. Both, so I was told, had been chosen for their size in order to give stability to the little cars rounding corners at racing speed. The rest of us, after an hour or two, wearied of keeping a tally of circuits completed by each car, and sought out the refreshment marquee. But nothing could budge Yeats from his seat and his score-sheet throughout the entire afternoon. Mrs Yeats had to feed him *in situ*.

*   *   *

But to return to the Abbey Theatre going-away party at the Gresham Hotel. When the time came for us all to depart, I made my way to the foyer to await Ria Mooney. I proposed to escort her home in a taxi. The foyer was occupied only by the solitary figure of Yeats. He was standing sipping from a glass of milk. I had been told that he was not in good health and had been put on to milk by his doctor. I didn't approach him; I was too much on edge lest the tall and handsome Norris Davidson should succeed in plucking away Ria Mooney from me. Norris Davidson was the Irish Cambridge graduate who made film documentaries and who had occupied rooms in the Oxford and Cambridge Mansions in the Euston Road area of London — the Mansions that Uncle Lennox had installed me in, prior to my escaping from them to Chelsea.

One of my chief buttresses against the unthinkable fate of losing Ria Mooney was Norris Davidson himself. I had got the impression that he was not a lady's man but, rather, a man's man. On the outbreak of war he had enlisted in the small Irish navy. Later, in his own boat, he was given to cruising the coasts of Ireland and thus visited my father, my mother and myself at 'Raffeen' in Kinsale. The hugely amorous Scottish Juno had somehow got separated from her mother and had to be seen home in another taxi. There was no one else available for the task except Norris or myself. Would sheer desperation cause the immensely civilised Norris's civilisation to crack, thus causing him to attempt to grab Ria Mooney from me? It was a nightmare thought. Although I suffered some qualms of conscience at my bare-faced attempt to lumber him with Juno, my single-minded commitment to getting Ria easily quelled my scruples. The two taxis were hailed. Ria was successfully manoeuvred towards mine, and Norris stood with Juno at the pavement's edge beside his. All seemed to be well.

Then my heart stopped. Norris was striding in our direction. Had his psyche collapsed under the strain? His face thrust forward, he hissed at us, 'For what we are about to receive, may the Lord make us truly thankful.' The next moment he was back again with Juno. The taxi engulfed them. I hoped that he would survive. But he had left Ria in stitches of laughter that continued even when we were being driven away. As every soundly educated person knows, a taxi is not a vehicle; it is a boudoir. But how could one be romantic with a lady who was laughing at a joke, worse still, at another man's joke? However, at last I got her settled down and together we listened to the rhythm of the universe.

If Ria Mooney was a powerful advocate of the Abbey Theatre style of acting, she was equally a denigrator of the film actor's claim to skill. When I acquainted that redoubtable film star, Laurence Olivier, with her views during a meeting with him at the Gresham Hotel (visiting notables nearly always seemed to stay at the Gresham Hotel, though I met the great Australian soprano Joan Hammond at the Shelbourne), his reaction was of the sharpest.

Ria Mooney had said to me, 'I've been asked if it's necessary to be a good stage actor in order to be a good film actor. My answer to that is: to be a success on the films it is not necessary to be able to act at all! Some of the screen's brightest stars couldn't act to save their lives. Given a dumb animal or a month- old baby, the combined efforts of film producer, camera man, cutter and script-writer will provide you with a first-class piece of film acting.'

Hilton Edwards had once made much the same point to me, but only in the matter of child actors. He spoke of seeing performances by children on the screen which they never could have sustained on the stage. 'In a film,' he said, 'they can be produced almost gesture by gesture.'

When I reported Ria Mooney's comments to Laurence Olivier, he replied, 'I disagree. Screen acting is not easy at all. It is true that in certain circumstances an ungifted person can pass on the screen, but this is true also of the stage. And their success, in both cases, is ephemeral. Occasionally various competitions are held to promote new aspirants to film honours on no other qualifications than looks. If such aspirants last the course, as Maureen O'Hara, winner of a "Dawn" beauty contest in Dublin, appears to be doing, then it merely means that they have been born with a certain amount of talent.

'The idea that the film industry finds its new blood almost exclusively from among the winners of beauty competitions is hopelessly out-of-date. New blood is found through the efforts of the talent scouts. They visit theatres, music halls, amateur theatricals, and anywhere else that opportunity offers. The film industry doubtless made a bad name for itself in the early days, but it takes itself very seriously indeed now, works tremendously hard, and has made enormous progress — progress which the stage has not made of recent years.'

I said that I always associated Ria Mooney and Shelah Richards with Uncle Lennox, Dolly and Sorrento Cottage; and I spoke of Shelah Richards as the producer of Anew McMaster in Jean Giraudoux's *Amphitryon 38* at the Olympia Theatre. Although Shelah Richards' name was often on my uncle and aunt's lips, my early memories of meeting her are few. I recall that Dublin Drama League production in the summer on the lawn of Sorrento Cottage, a Greek play, perhaps W. B. Yeats's *Oedipus the King*, in which the cast were dramatists like Yeats, Rutherford Mayne and Uncle Lennox, and the audience were actors. It was played against the marvellous backdrop of beautiful Dublin Bay. I have a memory of Shelah Richards, with the others, seated in the sunshine on the sloping lawn and looking down at the grassy 'stage' below. I have a memory of her and her then husband, the enormously tall Denis Johnston the dramatist, at a tea party there which extended itself from the drawing-room out through the wide-open French windows on to the lawn, and thence down the short cliff path to the rocky bathing-place below. Finally I met her when Michael Walsh and she were running a series of seasons at the Olympia Theatre.

Although she didn't come of a theatrical family in the immediate sense, she was a descendant of the well-known eighteenth-century actress Miss O'Neill, who later married, became Lady Beecher, and settled down outside Cork. Miss O'Neill was a contemporary of Edmund Keane and Mrs Siddons.

'As far as I can make out,' Shelah Richards said to me, 'Miss O'Neill never appeared in the famous Smock Alley Theatre in Dublin, but did most of her acting in London. The bent towards acting lay dormant in my family until it burst out again in myself and my niece, Geraldine Firzgerald.'

Geraldine Fitzgerald, a very beautiful girl, was a highly paid British film starlette until she later secured a contract to play leading roles in Hollywood films. She was also an accomplished stage actress, winning the Critics' Prize for the best performance in New York in 1943.

Violet, better known as Haggie, Campbell, sister to the then Lord Glenavy, was an excellent amateur actress. She used to get up shows in Greystones near Dublin. Shelah Richards lived as a child in Greystones and, with some of her friends, took part in these shows. A few years later she packed everything she possessed, told her father that she was, whether he liked it or not, going to London to learn to act, took rooms for a year the moment she arrived, entered for the examination of the Royal Academy of Dramatic Art — and was back home a week later, a bad fit of nerves having lost her the examination.

'The most ardent opponent to my taking up a theatrical career,' she said to me, 'was Geraldine Fitzgerald's father. Perhaps the subsequent behaviour of his own daughter was a judgment on him!'

'What happened then?'

'To my amazement I found myself cast for a part by the Dublin Drama League, which I had joined before going to London. The play was being produced by Lennox Robinson. At this time I had never met him; he was only an exalted name to me. The piece consisted of a very highbrow and outspoken little dialogue between a Greek shepherd and shepherdess. I had to read through its (to me) very brazen lines with a youth not much older than, and quite as mentally gawky as, myself. Somehow we staggered through it.'

After she had taken home her part to learn, she spent her time in an agony of vacillation. Should she ever be able to go through with it? At last she made up her mind that she must do so. This was her Great Opportunity. Besides, she could not let down this wonderful theatrical hero who had chosen her from all Dublin to play this part. She rode in the train from Greystones to Bray determined to sacrifice her morals to her career. At Bray station she was greeted by one of the porters. He had been an acquaintance of hers since early childhood. Handing her the few sheets of paper that were her part, which she had accidentally left in the carriage, he said with a fat wink, 'Hot stuff eh, Miss Shelah!'

'That,' said Shelah Richards, 'was the end. I went straight to the Abbey Theatre. I found Lennox Robinson in the wardrobe room at the top of a ladder, his head almost buried in red petticoats. "Mr

148

Robinson, I want to talk to you." He turned his head, lifted a corner of a red petticoat, and peered down. For ten minutes I stammered out apologies and explanations. I received no help from the Ladder, which remained silent. Finally the Ladder said, "Oh!" I crept out. My career was shattered. However, through the intercession of friends Lennox Robinson, who has been such a wonderful friend to me since, gave me a small part in another Drama League show.'

Shelah Richards happened, during a drama League rehearsal at the Abbey Theatre, to be telling some amateurs like herself the story of her London experience. Michael Dolan, who was assistant producer to the Abbey at that time, was listening. 'Oh, turned down by the R. A. D. A!' he exclaimed. 'In that case there must be something to you. There might be a part for you some time.' And that was really the beginning of her theatrical career. A week later, due to the illness of Eileen Crowe, she was, at three or four days' notice, playing 'Mary' in Sean O'Casey's *Juno and the Paycock*.

'To this day,' said Shelah Richards, 'it remains one of my favourite parts, though I've had rotten eggs thrown at me while playing it.'

'When? Where?'

'At the Palace Cinema in Cork, then used as a theatre or music-hall. In the interval between the second and third acts, we had heard that the occupants of the gallery were going to object to Mary's illegitimate offspring. The parish priest had come in back stage during the show and announced that the play could not continue in its present form. The company was under the guidance of Sarah Allgood. She went with him to the office to discuss what should be done.

'The bell to take the curtain up had rung three times before a whirlwind Sarah Allgood launched herself from the office door on to the stage. She ignored my feeble question, "What are you going to say?" My whole scene depended on her answer; my entire function was to announce to my fiance that I couldn't marry him because I was about to have a baby by another man. There was nothing for it but to listen to what Sarah Allgood was saying. I heard her announce to my fiance that I couldn't marry him because I had consumption. When she came off, I protested that it was absolutely useless my going on. But she pushed me forward. So there was nothing for it but to repeat to my fiance my inability to marry him because of consumption. I couldn't think further ahead in the dialogue, though I knew that there were plenty of pitfalls lying in wait. But I was saved from having to embark on this stormy passage by a crescendo of hoots, catcalls and rotten eggs from the gallery. They were not going to be robbed of their fun by the obvious tubercular subterfuge.'

Chapter Twelve
1,000 Dublin Horsemen Charge Laurence Olivier

To return to Dennis Barry! 'Then,' he had said, 'there is Eileen Crowe. I think of her just as a charming personality, with a laugh so infectious that I almost have been ashamed of myself while watching her on the stage, thinking I have been a nuisance to my neighbours.'

I too used to think of her as just a charming personality, playing rather insipid Irish heroines. When I met her and found out her own attitude to such heroines, and had seen her in two character parts, I knew that, given the material, she could be an actress of great power. She had always had a craze for the theatre. Mainly she haunted the Abbey, but attended the Gaiety too. One day she saw a newspaper advertisement for the Abbey School of Acting.

'So you entered?'

'Lennox Robinson and Arthur Shiels still laugh at the girl who came to the audition and asked, when requested to read something, "Will I do it with actions?" It was a play about Columcille which I had been taking part in at school, and I couldn't imagine myself reading it without actions.'

'And the actions were successful?'

'They must have been, for I was admitted to the school. In one way I was particularly lucky to have joined at that time, as most of the first company were away in America (it was the tour that saw the great success of Lennox Robinson's *The Whiteheaded Boy*). So in six weeks I found myself playing leading parts, which was probably very bad for me. It's better to start with small parts and learn your job that way. I was learning it backwards.'

'What first parts?'

'The very first was The Girl in Terence McSweeney's *The Revolutionists*. The second was Sarah Curran in Lennox Robinson's *The Dreamers*. In those days no play was allowed to run for more than two weeks, however successful. The only exception was Sean O'Casey's *Juno and the Paycock*, which ran for three weeks on its first production. It could have run for twelve months at that time. W. B. Yeats was very definite about the two-weeks rule.'

'What made him relax for "Juno"?'

'Well by Wednesday morning the theatre was booked out. Not a seat left for the remainder of the week. The theatre was besieged. They had to keep it on.'

'What were the press notices like?'

'Oh, terrific, terrific. His previous play *The Shadow of a Gunman* had caused quite a sensation and prepared people for "Juno". One of my favourite parts is Minnie Powell in the "Gunman". It is one of the few straight parts which have any character in them. Most playwrights fall down on them; they are generally insipid. For that reason I have always preferred character work.'

'Did you come much into contact with O'Casey at that time?'

'Oh yes. I was in the audience on the first night of *Shadow of a Gunman*. I went round to the Green Room wildly enthusiastic. I found Sean O'Casey sitting there very nervous. He was tremendously pleased when I told him of the great reception the play was getting. I think it's a pity he ever left Dublin. He seemed to lose touch with the people he understood and wrote about so perfectly.'

'Have you seen any of his later plays?'

'I saw his *Within the Gates* badly done in London, and superbly done in New York. I still don't think it's a patch on any of his earlier plays.'

'How about learning parts?'

'I should think that Lennox Robinson is about the easiest author to learn, of any Abbey dramatist. His dialogue is always so smooth and natural. Synge, on the other hand, is particularly difficult, and so is Lady Gregory.'

'I wonder if Dublin actors find difficulty in getting the accent and lilt of the western speech of Synge's characters?'

'There may be something in that. But Maureen Delany, who comes from Galway, also finds it hard to learn. The thing about Synge and Lady Gregory is that once you have learnt their lines you never forget them. Speaking of Irish accents, somewhere on the United States west coast we were talking to an American. After listening to us intently for a long time he suddenly exclaimed, "D'you know, I can understand you perfectly!"'

'Any other experiences in the States?'

'Most of our plays on that first Abbey tour were given in colleges. The greater part of the students had never seen a play of any kind and were most appreciative. One of the most enthusiastic audiences we ever played to was in the college for coloured students in Tusgegee, Alabama. They got every point in the two plays we did there, Lennox Robinson's *The Whiteheaded Boy* and *The Far-off Hills*. The coloured students' faces merged with the blackness of the auditorium, and it was an extraordinary experience to see nothing but rows of white teeth in the darkness. Whenever a laugh line came they jumped in the air with delight.'

'Anything else?'

'When we were going to Florida, the land of sunshine, we left all our winter things behind. But we arrived at Daytona beach to see the palm trees bending down nearly to the ground before the gale. The temperature was equivalent to that of an Irish November. We were frozen. In Hollywood we were feted. But it was a very different matter for players who went there looking for work. Among the "extras" acting in the picture we made of Sean O'Casey's *The Plough and the Stars* were film people who had once been world names.'

Maureen Delany, the leading Abbey Theatre comedienne, also described to me the manner in which they were feted. 'Dudley Digges, Robert Montgomery, Edward G. Robinson, James Cagny, Maureen O'Sullivan and Una O'Conner gave me many happy evenings in their homes. All the different stars from the various studios came to see us every night. One evening, when we were performing Synge's *The Playboy of the Western World*, we had Maureen O'Sullivan, James Cagney, Robert Montgomery and Ralph Bellamy walking on as supers with the crowd in the last act, so proud were they to be seen on the stage with the Abbey Theatre Company. That's what they thought of us in Hollywood.'

'Was it,' I asked Eileen Crowe,' the Abbey Theatre Company who made the film of *The Plough and the Stars?*'

'No, just five of us, Barry Fitzgerald, Arthur Shiels, Dennis O'Dea, Peter and myself. We were brought over specially by R. K. O. The director was John Ford.'

' "Peter and myself"! Who's Peter?'

'My husband, F. J. McCormick. His real name, you know, is Peter Judge.'

'Then are his initials "F. J." also part of the pseudonym?'

'Yes. He doesn't even know what they stand for! The initials of John McCormick, the great Irish tenor, are just the opposite way round, "J. F.". He always draws attention to it when introducing my husband to anyone. We spent some very pleasant hours in John McCormick's house in Hollywood. A wonderful place it was. So extensive were the grounds that we had to go by car from the house to the swimming pool and tennis courts.'

F. J. McCormick, destined to become one of Europe's very finest actors, didn't *go* on to the stage; he just wandered on to it more or less by chance. He was always intensely interested in the theatre — as a spectator. 'I wanted to look at the show, but I didn't want to be part of it. In a sense, that attitude remains with me still. Though I've played hundreds of parts during my years with the Abbey, I never was "dying down dead" to play any particular part. I just made the best job I could of whatever part I was given to do.'

It was this that developed in F. J. McCormick his astonishingly wide range. He went to no dramatic school beyond the school of the stage itself. At seventeen he joined the Workmen's Club in York Street, and there learnt his craft through a series of melodramas and one-act farces. His first professional performance was at the Queen's Theatre, and he was paid a pound for it. In 1919, at the Abbey Theatre, he began to live solely by the stage, giving up his job in the Civil Service.

I asked him what were the outstanding occasions in his career.

'Two of them. One was the first production of Sean O'Casey's *The Shadow of a Gunman.* At that time we were very close to the realities of bombs and raids and Black an'Tans. And nearer still to the bitterness of the Civil War. So O'Casey's comment on the

154

gunman was hard hitting at both sides, and a safety valve for the non-combatant members of the Abbey audiences.'

'And the second?'

'I recall with pleasure and pride the great personal interest of W. B. Yeats in my performance of Oedipus in his fine translation of Sophocles' classic. Almost night after night round to the dressing-room he would come. He would tell me where I had failed and where I was better than before and where I was to try for this and where I was to avoid that. Yeats knew what he wanted, and he didn't pretend to you that you'd got it. But he did encourage you to get as near to it as you could, and his enthusiasm and understanding made you do your damnedest. It wasn't Yeats's fault if your damnedest still left you no match for the Grecian giant.'

With conditions difficult in wartime Britain, a number of British film companies found the space, the 'extras' manpower then needed, and sometimes the scenery, in Ireland. Two of the film stars that crossed the Irish Sea, and whom I met on separate occasions, were Laurence Olivier, already established world-wide as a star of the screen quite apart from his repute as an actor on the stage; and Deborah Kerr, rapidly pushing her way into world-wide recognition. Ireland was apt to be used just for the exterior shots, while the interiors were filmed in the British studios.

Laurence Olivier had come to make his film of Shakespeare's *Henry V*. Deborah Kerr had come less prestigiously to make a 'thriller' called, *I Spy a Dark Stranger* (now re-titled, *I See a Dark Stranger*). Laurence Olivier, I would guess, had come over at least partly because he required a vast number of horsemen to simulate the charge of the French cavalry at the Battle of Agincourt against Henry V (played by himself) and his lethal bowmen. Deborah Kerr said she had come over because, quite simply, the scene of her film was laid in Ireland. Laurence Olivier was in both respects, film and stage, a mature actor. Deborah Kerr, I was told beforehand (not that either of these facts, if facts they were, emerged in our conversation), was only nineteen years of age and had made some reputation for herself on the boards of the Bristol Old Vic. Laurence Olivier's name I pronounced correctly. Deborah Kerr's (pronounced 'car' as in 'motor-car') I pronounced 'cur' throughout. How she summoned up the fortitude to be called a cur for over an hour without protest I can't imagine, unless she had suffered the same fate before from others and had become inured. Perhaps it was just youthful diffidence and sheer good manners. Laurence Olivier had a wealth of theatrical and cinematic experience and deduction to bring into the conversation. Deborah Kerr, still near the dawn of her career, stuck to biographical facts. Laurence Olivier's filming was done outside Dublin. Important scenes in Deborah Kerr's were done within.

The charge of the French cavalry was shot, I was told, at Lord Powescourt's estate. County Dublin was scoured for horsemen. A thousand of them, said my informant, were raised. Railings were removed to leave an uninterrupted space for a half-mile rail- track. The camera was mounted upon a carriage running on the rails. As the charge took place, the camera was drawn away before it by a motor, and so the galloping horses were filmed.

Deborah Kerr was playing the part of the Irish heroine (she liked, she said, doing accents) who arrives in Dublin at Kingsbridge station, as it was then called. As I spoke to her in the Gresham Hotel, where we were photographed together, she was due shortly at the station. She was in her costume, fishnet stockings (I imagine they photographed out as coarse-woven and countrified rather than sexy), a tweed costume, and a hat to match. The scene, she said, was to be shot by a camera hidden inside a van with its back doors left open. It was the only way to stop a crowd's forming; the sight of a film camera always drew a crowd. 'There is also in the story a portrait gallery. For that we shall shoot the exterior of some imposing building in the city that might pass for a gallery. We also have some nice locations down in Wicklow. We're doing just the exteriors in Ireland. The rest will be done in the studios in Denham.'

The film was being made in black and white, as so many major films still were. I was told that the number of Technicolor cameras available for hire outside the United States was extremely limited. The other forms of colour photography available, I found poor by comparison. Where only black and white registered, the facial make-up was yellowish or sandy-hued. With Technicolor, a rather paler version of ordinary street make-up was employed. The camera tended to pick out pinks with too much emphasis. Consequently these colours in particular had to be muted. 'All the women on the set,' remarked Deborah Kerr, 'looked like consumptives.'

From school days, she had always wanted to act. Her aunt, a very talented woman, would have been a fine actress had she not elected to lead a family life. 'She taught me all I know. I've never been to a dramatic academy. She taught elocution at my school. She also had a small dramatic school to which I went later. We did plays and mimes for local charities.'

Shortly after this, Deborah Kerr got the notion that she would like to be a dancer. She travelled to London and enrolled at Sadler's Wells. The notion was brief-lived. She returned to drama, performing walk-ons for the Regents Park Open-air Theatre. The advent of war drove her back to her home near Bristol. After fretting and fuming for a while, she was back in London doing the round of the theatrical agents.

'One day,' she said, 'I was lunching with a friend at the Mayfair Hotel. The famous producer Gabriel Pascal was lunching there too. He knew my friend and came over to speak to her. Almost after the manner of the story-book great impressario he said to me, "I'll give you a test for Jennie in Shaw's *Major Barbara*." '

She had never so much as thought of films for herself before. She had expected to 'slave her way through repertory' for years to come. Films, to her, were something for the very elect and the very beautiful. She got the part. *Major Barbara* was the only picture being made in England in 1940, as France was falling and everything seemed to be in chaos.

She enjoyed her first experience of film-making not at all. In fact, she vowed that she would never go into a film studio again. The business seemed to consist of everybody's yelling at her and telling her to do this and that. It appeared impossible to do all the technical things required of her, and at the same time to remember her words and the part she was playing. 'By the end of it, I felt convinced that I was thoroughly bad.'

'Hardly that! In no time at all you were back in *Love On the Dole*.'

'Yes. Having been hit in the face as Jennie in *Major Barbara* by the Cockney Tough, played by Robert Newton; again hit in the face as Sally Hardcastle in *Love On the Dole* by the Father, played by George Carney; I was next cast for the role of Mary Brodie in *Hatter's Castle* in which I was again hit by my Father, played by Robert Newton.'

'And now here's another of your films, *The Life and Death of Colonel Blimp*, coming to Dublin!'

'Also I've only just finished, with Robert Donat, *Perfect Strangers*. We did it for Sir Alexanda Korda. It took a year.'

The tremendous publicity given by the cinema to young actors could also serve as a shortcut to leading parts on the stage, in a way that 'slaving through repertory' could never have accomplished. Deborah Kerr found herself playing at the Cambridge Theatre in Shaw's *Heartbreak House* with three of the most famous artists of the stage, Edith Evans, Robert Donat and Isobel Jeans. On going abroad with ENSA to perform before the troops, she filled the role of Mrs Manningham in *Gaslight*. Of course she had her own great ability to thank too. In Hollywood, as the years passed, she never lost her position near the head of the hierarchy.

But to return to Laurence Olivier. I have indicated on an earlier page the heat, or perhaps 'controlled warmth' would be a more accurate phrase, with which he rebutted Ria Mooney's strictures on the art, or lack of it, of the film actor. I was talking to him in the sitting-room of his suite at the Gresham Hotel. Its window was closed against the rattle and clanging of the trams entering into, and emerging from, the tangle of lines round the base of the as yet unblown-up Nelson's Column in O'Connell Street that formed the terminus. I took in his appearance with interest. Though I knew of his reputation as a stage actor, I had seen him, often in giant close-up, only on the screen. He was just as handsome off it, but looked a little older, his hair touched with grey.

In the current issue of my theatre (and cinema) monthly *Commentary*, I had begun a series under the title of *Questionnaires to Celebrities*. First of the celebrities to be questioned was Micheal MacLiammoir. *Inter alia* he had remarked, while stating that some intelligence was required for acting, 'An overplus of intelligence is fatal to the actor. I myself could never act even as well as I do, were it not for the cavities with which nature has so thoughtfully pitted my intellect.'

Laurence Olivier had seen the issue. 'I think that MacLiammoir is being unduly modest, having regard to his talent and his intelligence, both of which reach an unusual degree of overplus.' He glanced at me with a smile. 'Compliment to a fellow artist!'

My first fleeting thought (it was *only* a first thought and a *very* fleeting one) was that Laurence Olivier was being gracious in treating Micheal MacLiammoir as an equal. It was a bit like Goliath, at least before the battle, referring to David as a military colleague. My thought was in no way derogatory to MacLiammoir. It was only that I had in mind, in those pre-television days of crowded cinemas, the vast power of the industry to build up within months the reputation of a film star on a world-wide scale. No stage actor, however skilled, could compete in that respect.

I myself received, for my magazine cover, free full-page colour printing 'blocks', costing sums beyond my reach, bearing photo-portraits of stars, generally female, in glamorous poses. The cover of a magazine is its shop-window, its greatest selling factor. The first time I used one of these blocks, the magazine was sold out almost at mid-month. On the spot, I put up my next printing order by fifty per cent. Papier-maché moulds were also showered upon me. Into these, molten lead could be poured and 'stereos' cheaply produced, bearing smaller pictures complete with caption to decorate my pages. Kees van Hoek, a well-known Dutch journalist working first for *The Irish Independent* and then for *The Irish Times*, twitted me on my 'filmic young ladies'. But, running the magazine as I was on a shoestring, I was glad of help from any quarter. Also, I enjoyed looking at the filmic young ladies.

My second and almost instant thought was that Laurence Olivier was first and foremost an artist of the stage, an intelligent and sensitive man who would care everything for quality and give small thought to quantity, who would be regarding Micheal MacLiammoir as a fellow actor, and a very good one, upon the boards.

Micheal MacLiammoir's relative by marriage, the Shakespearean actor Anew McMaster, would sometimes cross to England to take small parts under another name in films. This he did with the object of raising money to mount the theatrical productions that he cared about. 'Laurence Olivier,' he had said to me, 'does rather the same.'

Laurence Olivier confirmed this, though of course he was playing leading roles under his own name. 'The theatre was my first love. Quite frankly, I looked upon films as a way of making money in order to do what I wanted in the theatre. I didn't believe in them at that time. Ten years have passed, ten years that have shown me that the screen is a very exact science allowing of no mistakes, ten years that have greatly developed it as an art form until now I do believe in it.'

Anew McMaster himself had a great regard for the cinema. 'Has it ever struck the public that the music, often quite magnificent, played through a film renders it melodrama in the old sense, that is, drama with music? If I ever produced *Romeo and Juliet*, I should have it produced practically as music drama; I should have an undercurrent of music played right through it. The highbrows would say that this was cheap. There is nothing cheap about it. One wouldn't do it in Ibsen's *Ghosts*, or in any other very realistic modern play. But, in emotional drama, it's a great help. This is one direction in which the modern stage might well copy the films.'

There were other directions ('technical showman ways') in which the cinema influenced the theatre. It speeded things up; no longer was it acceptable to have long waits and intervals. Wigs on the films were works of art. Theatrical wigs greatly improved. The prices of seats at the Dublin Gaiety Theatre in the forties were practically the same as they had been seventy years previously despite the rise in the cost of living. The competition of the cinema had kept them down.

'It shows,' remarked Anew McMaster, 'how firmly the theatre is founded, that it has been able to stand up against the cheap entertainment of the cinema. The latter is warm, it's comfortable, it's fast-moving and soothing. It doesn't call for the intellectual effort of the theatre. As Mr. de Valera said to me the other day, after watching a performance of *Hamlet*, "The film is soporific; the theatre is stimulating."'

That, of course, was in the forties. *The Clockwork Orange* and *The Exorcist*, among many others, would hardly allow the cinema any longer to qualify as a haven of mental rest!

But to return once more to my conversation with Laurence Olivier in his rooms at the Gresham Hotel. 'I think,' he said, 'that the stage has very little reason to adopt the pompous attitude towards the films that it sometimes does adopt. The actor who graduates successfully from the stage to the screen finds it exceedingly difficult

160

to adjust himself and his technique to the new conditions. It is a much smaller medium than the stage. Being a smaller medium, it is much more difficult to control the difference between good and bad. Mistakes show up more sharply. The stage actor reaches for larger dimensions. While it is possible to give a greater performance on the stage than it is on the screen, small slips are not so acutely accentuated in the theatre. It would be difficult for the greatest actor in the world to be better than Gary Cooper on the screen, but he would be capable of giving a greater performance on the stage than the screen could ever hope to equal.'

He pointed to the fine Irish stage actors, Barry Fitzgerald and Thomas Mitchell, who had continued to do good work when transplanted to Hollywood. ('There's no doubt that Ireland produces excellent actors.') As for those screen actors who hadn't previous experience of the stage, who started off in the films from scratch, it couldn't be said of them that their work wasn't acting. It was just another kind of acting, one just as difficult to do as anything else in the world which hadn't previousby been tried.

This point about the difference in size between the two media was also made to me by Sybil Thorndike. I had asked her if, during her career, she had noticed any general change (up to the forties) in the style of acting.

'The tendency which has come from the pictures of getting everything smaller and smaller and more naturalistic. So much so that in some of the theatres you can't hear what the players are saying at all. To be naturalistic doesn't mean to be more real. But the public, from their training at the films, like something that is photographically exact.'

'Are you in sympathy with this trend?'

'No. I'm not. The logical conclusion of this is the films, which is another art. I think that the theatre has gradually decayed from Elizabethan times.'

Apart from this general change in taste, she had found audiences in certain places quicker in their reactions than others. The Welsh were very quick. Anything Celtic she found more responsive. She had discovered this from her recent playing to Welsh miners. She felt that audiences in big towns tended to be the same. They got the same films, used the same make-up, dressed in the same clothes. They

161

were much less individualised than they used to be. 'Individuality is the most marvellous thing in the world, yet they all want to be alike.'

'What of films from the point of view of the art of the actor?'

'They are a frightful danger to any but a real actor who knows exactly what he is doing. Their effect on the young and inexperienced actor is to make him so much under-act, that he becomes useless for the theatre. For the theatre, people have to be ten times larger than life size. For the films, because of the magnification, they have to be smaller. Actors of less vitality are less effective on the stage, but more effective on the screen. I can't imagine Edith Evans on the films. I think she'd bust them!'

Laurence Olivier had felt bad about being away in the United States during the first fearful year of Hitler's bombing of Britain, and had wanted to return to join the Royal Air Force as a pilot. Any British criticism of his absence was stilled when Churchill, desperate for American help, let it be known that he had blocked Olivier's immediate return, preferring to have him where he might perhaps plead Britain's cause. When at length he was permitted to return with his wife Vivien Leigh, star, in the role of Scarlett O'Hara, of that immense Hollywood film *Gone With the Wind*, he joined the Air Force and was posted in 1942 to Worthy Down. While there, he was asked to play the title role in a radio version of Shakespeare's *Henry V*, being broadcast as a wartime morale booster.

Filippo del Giudice heard the broadcast. An Italian immigrant, he was one of a number of foreigners who had become prime movers in building up the British film industry. To this end, he had joined forces with the flour millionaire, J Arthur Rank. When war broke out, del Giudice was interned as the citizen of an enemy country. Shortly after, he was released on the condition that he would devote himself to making morale boosting films. *Henry V*, dealing as it did with a great English (and Welsh!) victory, seemed ideal. He contacted Laurence Olivier to play the title role again, in a film version. Olivier received the offer with little enthusiasm. He felt that other efforts to transfer Shakespeare on to film had ended in failure. But his wife, Vivien Leigh, wanting to divert him from his attempts to get transferred to a war zone, pressed him to accept. She found an ally in the distinguished actor, Ralph Richardson.

Ralph Richardson, agreeing that Shakespeare on film had hitherto been a failure, asked Olivier how he would do it. The reply filled him with enthusiasm. He urged him to demand from del Giudice full control over script, music, lighting, camera and acting. Instead of the expected explosion, he got a full acceptance. In drafting the script with the help of a writer, Olivier built the star role of the French princess Katherine round Vivien Leigh. Word of this got out. Vivien Leigh was under contract to David Selznick . A series of cables threatening injunctions arrived from Hollywood. Finally del Giudice succeeded in his pleas that Vivien should be dropped; he needed the American market if the film was to succeed.

A little known actress, Renee Anderson, was substituted. While naturally delighted, she never concealed from herself that she had been chosen because she had the same measurements as Vivien Leigh; all the costumes had already been made. Vivien Leigh never forgave Selznick for obstructing her appearing with Laurence Olivier. (Even in *Gone With the Wind* she had wanted to appear opposite him, but Clark Gable was preferred.) She represented to herself as a persecution Selznick's threats of an injunction. She decided to spend the time, while the film was being made, having the child that Laurence Olivier and she had always wanted. But instead there was a miscarriage. Added to this was the ever greater withdrawal of her husband from her, due to the immensity of the task he had undertaken. Even in her schooldays there had been shifts of personality which doubtless today would have been recognised for what they were. When her final mental collapse came, it was total.

As for Laurence Olivier, exhausted by the enormous effort that he had put into every aspect of the filming, and too close to it to realise that he had constructed a screen masterpiece, his only sentiment was expressed in the words, 'Never again!'

Chapter Thirteen
Uncle Lennox Again

Although the events that I have recounted took place in the twenties, the thirties, the forties, for me this private era of mine ended only in the sixties, because an era is determined by persons rather than by dates. The people of the older generation who made it for me were my father and mother, my Uncle Tom and Aunt Ethel, and Uncle Lennox. It was my father and mother who took me to India and points on the way; to Italy, to Switzerland, and to France. It was they who sent me to Castle Park Preparatory School, to St. Columba's College and to Oxford. It was Uncle Tom and Aunt Ethel who provided my sisters and myself with our stable home when our parents were in India. It was Uncle Lennox who injected the excitements into my adolescence and early adulthood by introducing me into the world of the theatre. And they all died about the same time. It was their deaths that closed the door.

In my first chapter I wrote, 'Uncle Lennox adored my mother. Delicate as a child, he was omitted by his three brothers from their games. ("Gates shut in my face" I remember was the phrase he used.) My mother, sharing his interest in writing, music and painting, was his childhood companion.' I might have added that my mother told me that, at such times as he was adjudged too delicate to attend Bandon Grammar School, he shared with her the teaching of her governess.

The closing of the door is symbolised for me by a window in the side chapel of St. Multose in Kinsale. The ponderous twelfth-century church contains many memorials to my family. The large and appalling East Window with its bunches of flowers, a momument to bad taste and 'low' church principles (perish the thought that any symbol or figure might be admitted into it which might cause the foolish to worship it in the idolatrous fashion of those benighted Roman Catholics!), was erected by Dormans. The money raised by the sale of my paternal grandfather's stamp collection furnished the money which enabled my father to arrange for the reconstruction of the chancel ceiling.

The three stained-glass windows in the side chapel, infinitely better and replete with figures, were erected by Dormans, two of them by my father. The second of these latter he commissioned to the memory of my mother. Knowing of the closeness that had subsisted between her and her brother Lennox Robinson, he included his name. Before the window could be erected, he himself was dead. My sisters and I had a tablet placed beneath it dedicating it to the memory of all three of them.

What *was* the nature of this closeness between my Uncle Lennox and my mother? I had always assumed that it was due to the delicacy which had often obliged him to share her governess. I had also assumed that it was due to his rejection by his brothers. I have recently discovered that matters were by no means so simple. Indeed at one period she too rejected him, and at another he hated her!

In 1938 the London publishers Michael Joseph brought out a book entitled *Three Homes*. It was written jointly by my mother Nora Dorman, my Uncle Tom Robinson, and my Uncle Lennox Robinson. Each in turn contributed memories of their three homes in County Cork, and Lennox edited the material to form a coherent narrative. I read the book at the time of its publication, but only with the eyes of a man in his twenties. Now I have read it again after a longer experience of life, and with eyes able to penetrate a little deeper. Suddenly small episodes between my Uncle Lennox and myself take on a new significence, as the background of his upbringing is unrolled before me.

Was his later alcoholism attributable to rejection in childhood? But there was no rejection — by his elders. Rather the contrary. My mother writes, 'I was no favourite of hers.' (Mrs Coleman, their nurse.) 'Her pet was our youngest — Lennox. Me she regarded as a nuisance. Girls were always a mistake, boys in every way superior, and even one girl in a family of five was one too many.' And again, Lennox himself writes, 'They' (his brothers Arthur and Tom) 'despised me because I was petted by my mother and Miss Lewis' (a later governess). 'I remained at home, being considered too young and delicate for school, taught by Miss Lewis, and when she left us, my mother and my sister became my teachers. My mother loved teaching and I loved to learn from her. My father taught me Latin. I got thrown back on my mother and on older people. Years afterwards, when I began to write, it was evident that one of the few things I could do well was to write the thoughts of middle-aged and ordinary people. I am sure that this is because through all my childhood I had no friends of my own age.' His mother of course would have noticed his inability to relate to his generation. One of her favourite sayings to him was, 'A man that hath friends must show himself friendly.' Lennox comments, 'I did not show myself friendly.'

His rejection by his brothers and sister was almost complete. He writes, 'Between a child of six' (himself) 'and a boy' (Monty, the eldest of the family) 'of fourteen a gulf exists and, for the first few years at Kinsale he and my sister scarcely existed for me; they dwelt apart on Olympian heights. But only two and four years separated me from Arthur and Tom — yet there again was a gulf. They would have nothing to do with me. I daresay I was whining and difficult, but their ostracism made me more difficult; made me, in the end, different.' When Miss Lewis the governess departed, and his education had to be undertaken by his family, he records, 'My sister taught me French and Arithmetic and we hated each other.' And again, 'My brothers quickly found friends of their own age. I was the younger, the puling hanger-on. There were expeditions when I was deliberately left behind, excursions on which I would be enticed behind barred gates and there imprisoned.'

Were, then, his brothers and sister a race of ogres? Of course not. No one ever had a more gentle and loving mother than I, nor nicer uncles than Monty and Tom. (Arthur, killed fighting in the First World War, I never met.) It is just that children can be, by turns, adorable and monsters; and Lennox, I don't doubt, was very trying.

During the summers in Kinsale, things were somewhat better. He was included in the picnics and bathing parties and, as he grew older, was allowed to take the train to the next station outside the town. There he spent the afternoon in a wood through which ran a stream.

But his rejection recommenced when he joined the evening train, bringing his brothers Tom and Arthur home from school in Cork. 'It was an understood thing that I must not speak to them or expect to be recognised in any way.' Also it was unfortunate, when it came to tennis, to be the youngest in a family of five. A foursome could be made up without him. 'When the spate of Dorman relations arrived, the chances of an eleven- or twelve-year-old grew very slender. At large tennis parties I was put to field balls.' In the winter there were afternoon walks for him with my mother and a girl friend of hers. But their talk was of matters that he either didn't understand or didn't care about. He lagged behind them, his 'boots thick with the limestone mud of the Kinsale roads', his 'feet aching with chilblains'.

Chilblains! What of his health? Was this a factor in the later addiction to alcohol? My mother writes of 'Lennox thin and delicate looking and blue with cold, for he felt cold much more than we did.' Lennox himself writes, 'Within a few weeks of our arrival at Ballymoney' (the third of the 'Three Homes' in County Cork described in the joint book) 'I went to school for the first time. My brother Arthur and I travelled each morning by train to Bandon, twelve miles away, to attend the Grammar School there. It was a happy year for me, but only a year. I suffered from a succession of terrible headaches. I was growing too fast. If I did catch an infection, I would have no stamina to fight for life. So school had to come to an end, and for more than two years I had to lounge at home.' At a much later period my mother writes of him as 'taller and thinner than ever.' Lennox himself gives his height as six foot seven, and his weight as only nine stone. This height comes as a great surprise to me. I had set him down in my mind as being about six foot three. But he didn't hold himself straight, his mien perhaps being best described as 'droopy'!

My mother told me that he had had trouble with his eyes. At one period it was prescribed that he lie in a darkened room for several hours each day. Certainly he was the only one of the Robinsons who wore glasses when young. He was short sighted. This I, who also suffer from myopia, learned on the occasion when he took me as a schoolboy to a cinema, and he kindly lent me his glasses, I having forgotten to bring my own. Myopia alone, especially if accompanied by astigmatism, would account for headaches. I remember my own at the end of each day of a glaring sun, during my second visit to India. And this despite my wearing the darkest sunglasses that could be purchased. But when, on my return to Ireland, my vision was corrected by spectacles, the headaches became a thing of the past.

'A man that hath friends must show himself friendly.' Lennox as a boy, wounded by many snubs and left without hope, may not have shown himself friendly to his coevals. But, for me, there was no hint of this in Lennox the man. In middle age he greatly enjoyed the company of young men: myself, Norris Davidson, a number of others. So much so that at one time I wondered, despite his relationship with Dolly, whether there were not in his make-up at least elements of homo- sexuality, though most certainly not in the form of any physical outlet. But it occurred to me that it might result in a certain sexlessness. Such plays of his as I had seen did indeed show a delicate comedy understanding of women. But I felt that there it ended; that he had no power or insight to thrust his way into the passions and frustrations of the bedchamber.

Then I remembered the occasion when I had visited him in his box at the Gaiety Theatre, and he had rapped me over the knuckles for having, with Margaret, closed down the Picture Hire Club so abruptly. The box had been filled with lady friends of his own age. I remembered, at a time when his effective day was closing in and ever shortening, as it does for so many alcoholics, the astonishing clarity and authority with which, it being early, he conducted a committee meeting — of women. For a moment I glimpsed the Lennox that had been the young Manager of the Abbey Theatre. So he could show himself friendly both to young men and older women!

What of older men and younger women? No trouble there. W. B. Yeats, Rutherford Mayne, Sean O'Casey, T. S. Eliot, Lord Longford, Barry Fitzgerald, Arthur Shiels; Ria Mooney, Sheila Richards, Eileen Crowe, Maureen Delaney, the two young American girls laughing at every remark that he made in the coffee bar of the Abbey Theatre — he took them all in his stride. He clearly loved his Irish Drama lecture tours in the United States, the Abbey Theatre Company following in his wake to illustrate them; and the reception afterwards which ended in an orgy of hand shaking. He laughed at this last in his play, *Ever the Twain*. The American hand-shakers were represented by cardboard cut-outs, which gave some offence across the Atlantic.

What of children? Perhaps not quite so good there, though most certainly not bad. He said to me in later years, speaking of the occasions when he had taken me out from Castle Park Preparatory School for artificial-cream cakes in Dalkey, 'We never knew what to say to one another.' He could easily have broken through the wall of my shyness if, instead of observing me with a quizzical expression as I ploughed my way through pastry after pastry, he had descended from his grown-up heights and entered into my eleven-year-old world. There he could have explored with me my passion for drawing mazes, then all the rage at the school; my fear of French verbs, my happiness, while lying on my rug watching an inter-school first-eleven cricket match, in making lemonade by putting lemon crystals into water grown luke warm in a tin can under a summer sun; my misery as the headmaster once again held me up to ridicule before the whole school at Assembly, because of my latest absent-minded blunder. But Uncle Lennox was my Fairy Godfather just the same.

Perhaps his alcoholism was due, not to his inability to relate, but to his ability to relate too well. His very gregariousness would bring him into contact with hard drinkers, a species not unknown in Ireland, and not impossible to find in the United States. He was a brave man, but one very highly strung. However sober, his long thin hands tended to tremble a little. He could hardly have felt within himself any robustness of health. Perhaps drink, so fatal in the end, gave him the support he needed at the time.

From such an unpromising beginning, how was it that he came eventually to adore my mother? And what was his emotional relationship with this Stewart Dorman who later put up the stained-glass window in St. Multose Church in Kinsale to the memory of them both? Lennox writes, 'Another thing that made me happy was my friendship with Nora. She no longer taught me French and Arithmetic, and when Arthur entered a bank and Tom was teaching in England and her beloved Monty had gone to South Africa, we discovered that we could like each other. We read the same books, occasionally went to the theatre in Cork. We tried to

169

write. Flora Cornwall and I started a monthly magazine called *Contributions*. Nora's contributions were among the best, and from a short story of hers I made my first little play. But this good time had to come to an end. The Stewart Dorman so adored by me as a child took Nora to India as his wife. I felt that we had nurtured a viper for all those years.' My mother writes, 'Lennox and I were alone at Ballymoney, and it was then that the gap between our ages seemed to close and we became friends. We both loved books and we both began to write. The old crowded family life of us all together was for ever finished, and where should I have been but for this dear youngest brother.'

Other memories come to me with a new significance, not only from reading *Three Homes*, but also from the pages of Dr. Michael J. O'Neill's biography, *Lennox Robinson*. Even as I write with my pen those words, 'Lennox Robinson', I stare at them, startled. For — I am gazing straight at my dead uncle's signature! His family genes, passed to me through his sister my mother, surviving in concrete form into the future? It never before occurred to me, it doesn't occur to me now, that my writing is like his, except when I write his actual name. Oh, it isn't like his signature in his later years, when it degenerated into little more than an L followed by an almost straight line, and an R similarly followed. But I feel myself to be looking at the more readable signature of an earlier time. I have had a similar experience on another occasion. Often, as I sat writing on the sofa at 'Lackaroo' in Crosshaven, or on that of 'Raffeen' in Kinsale, my mother would be reading a French novel (for she always kept up her French), or perhaps a novel by Dickens or Jane Austen. From time to time she would quietly clear her throat. The other day, while working, I cleared my own. The manner and timbre of my doing it was so exactly like hers, that I looked up quickly, almost expecting to find her sitting once again beside me.

Of Kinsale she writes, 'There were happy days in Kinsale, but somehow the general impression of those seven years is not happy, and I should never wish to live them again. Westgrove — yes — Ballymoney — yes — but five Fisher Street — ten thousand times no.' Often, in later years, she told us of the dentist with his surgery opposite and, in those days before anaesthetics, of the screams of his patients as he extracted their teeth. Elsewhere she writes, 'We lived at Number Five, in Number Six lived deaf and alarming old Dr. Dorman our landlord, in Number Seven lived a large tribe of other Dormans. The only point on which I personally remember quarrelling with the Dorman girls, Eza and Cossie, was the rival merits of our elder brothers. For my elder brother, Monty, was my hero and my dearest, and it was more than I could bear to hear them brag of an older step-brother, Stewart, who was, they declared, bigger, stronger, cleverer, superior in every way.' Strange irony, eventually to marry this same Stewart — my father!

Other pictures flash upon the screen of my mind. Of Ballymoney Rectory Lennox writes, 'The Connors were the squires of the parish; their gracious house, Manch, was the only big house in our parish, if one excepts Kilcascan Castle, where lived the Catholic O'Neill Daunts.' My father took me, as a child, to Manch one day, and for the first time I saw a grown man weeping. It was the early days of Ireland's independence, and nationalist irregulars were burning the houses of many of the Protestant Anglo-Irish. Mr Connor's house itself had escaped, but he showed us the chared remains of his outhouses and his car.

Coming back from India at the age of nine, I naturally missed much of the lives of my grandparents. Indeed I never was aware of my paternal grandfather. He died in the same year that I was born. Perhaps the event proved too much for him! But, fleeting though the impression was, I saw enough of my maternal grandfather to have realised his charm, his goodness and his self effacement. Without being able to lay claim to his great human qualities, I was yet delighted to find that there was something of him in myself. One day, cycling along with my mother at Crosshaven, I uttered some whimsy that had come into my mind. 'You sound,' she said, 'exactly like my father!'

This same habit of uttering, on the spur of the moment, un-considered whimsicalities, led me into some small trouble with Uncle Lennox. Never, in my long periods of staying with Lennox and Dolly at Sorrento Cottage, did I ever notice the smallest hint of religiousness on the part of either. Indeed before their marriage they 'lived in sin', to use Uncle Lennox's own expression humorously uttered. Never did they go to church. Never did they give utterance to any religious sentiment. There is a poem by Dante Gabriel Rossetti which contains

171

the two lines, 'The blessed damozel leaned out — From the gold bar of Heaven.' One day I suddenly announced, with nothing particular in mind and to nobody in particular, 'The blessed damozel leaned out of the bar.'

'Don't blaspheme!' Uncle Lennox looked really shocked. 'That's blasphemy!'

I was surprised to learn, after his death, that he had a connection with an Actors' Church Union. Indeed Dr. Michael O'Neill records, in his biography, that Lennox actually founded this in 1947. Now that I think of it, was not the psychiatrist who attempted to wean him from his drink a minister of religion? The influence of a well loved clergyman father had not been without its effect!

At Christmas there would be an exchange of visits. Uncle Lennox would ascend from the bus to Uncle Tom and Aunt Ethel at their large farm house in the mountains at Glencullen, bearing presents for my sisters and myself. A day or two later, on Christmas Day itself, Uncle Tom would motor, myself with him, down to Dalkey on the sea. After dinner with Lennox and Dolly, Uncle Tom would have a couple of glasses of whisky, almost his only drinks in the course of a year. When the time came for the King's Christmas Day message to the British Commonwealth, the radio would be switched on for Tom's benefit. As the orchestra struck up the British National Anthem, Uncle Tom would advance towards the radio set and stand rigidly to attention with his back presented to us. The Irish-nationalist Lennox, giggling behind his long bony hand, would remain seated by the fire with Dolly and myself. I assumed at the time that Uncle Tom's behaviour was dictated solely by the fact that, as a captain in the Royal Munster Fusiliers, he had borne the King's commission. After re-reading *Three Homes* recently, I have begun to wonder whether there was not even more to it than that.

Lennox writes of his older brothers Tom and Arthur, as teenagers in Kinsale: 'They disliked her' (Miss Lewis the governess) 'very much, and nearly every night in our bedroom a strange scene would take place. I would be in bed and nearly asleep, when my brothers would come to bed and, while they undressed, they would unfold to each other Miss Lewis's crimes during the day. They seemed in perfect accord, my brothers, but suddenly, surprisingly, to my mind without

172

reason, they would begin to differ, at first politely, then rudely, finally they would end in a hand to hand fight, in a rolling over and over on beds and floor. I was never involved; I lay in bed trembling and speechless until at last the candle was blown out and one of them — probably Arthur the younger — sobbed himself to sleep. There was no innate antagonism there, for when they grew up they became the firmest of friends.'

I remember my Aunt Ethel once saying to me, 'When I feel like having a good row with your Uncle Tom, he'll never respond. He told me that he is afraid of losing his temper, because he once very nearly strangled Arthur.' Was Uncle Tom, as he stood, a solitary figure, stiffly to attention before the radio in the drawing-room of Sorrento Cottage, paying silent homage also to the memory of the brother whom he had so nearly strangled, and who had died as a young officer serving the same monarch as himself?

As to my maternal grandmother, I saw more of her, but never felt the slightest bit drawn to her. She had more to do with my sisters when we were children. But the only news of her that I can recall their bringing to me was to laugh at her for calling the toilet pedestal 'the Throne'; and for a constantly reiterated, 'I can hear a fly crawling on a window pane.' It came to me therefore with something of the force of a surprise to read in *Three Homes* of the love which the authors had for her. But really, it should have been no surprise to learn that three children, Tom, Nora and Lennox, loved their mother!

Lennox writes, 'Father's end at eighty-three' (Dr. Michael O'Neill gives it as seventy-nine) 'was rapid and comparatively painless. Mother's, ten years later in her eighty-second year, was long drawn out. But Nora hurried back from India to be with her in my house, Tom was only a mile or two away, and on a still April evening, the garden gay with the spring flowers she loved and the blackbirds and thrushes singing their maddest, her last words to us were, "Good night, dear children." '

That is the end as it should have been, as my mother and Uncle Lennox deserved to have it after their long and faithful vigil. I had been brought in to see 'Granny', looking grey, before my return for my next term at Oxford. But, to my mother's great distress, leaving Granny in good nursing hands, she and Uncle Lennox had taken a rare evening off to see a performance at the Abbey Theatre — and on that evening, in their absence, their mother died. I replied from England to my mother's letter, offering what comfort I could. They both deserved better.

Chapter Fourteen
Death of The Beloved

Both my mother's and father's deaths seemed to me to fit their lives.

My mother was artistic, sensitive, fastidious. She clung to her youth to the last. To the ways and pastimes of her beloved childhood, spent in a country rectory, she clung also, not only in the matters of her religion, and of her love of literature, painting, music; but also in those of her winter cold baths, of her sea-bathing from early spring to late autumn, her tennis until she had to lay down her racquet, the growing cataract in one eye making it increasingly difficult to gauge the speed and direction of the ball. She was self-effacingly devoted to her family.

Just as self-effacing seemed to me to be the moment of her death, as though she had chosen the one that would cause the least inconvenience to everybody. She had got our summer holiday visit home, that she always made so wonderful, safely over; she had written her usual letter saying how empty and dismal the house seemed to be without us (and certainly the world is empty and dismal without *her*), and then she left Kinsale and went off to her operation at the Dublin hospital where my younger sister Maureen and her husband worked as doctors. It was perhaps not a major operation, but she was, according to my guess, for she never revealed her age to me, in her seventies. At a later time my father showed me a flurry of letters written from the hospital. Every word in them was directed to one end solely, to making light of her discomforts and to reassuring him as to the speed of her recovery. To myself she didn't write at all until the operation was safely over, as it seemed, and then only in the vaguest terms. On such occasions she had but one instinct towards her children; they must be protected from all avoidable worry.

If she had seen to it that her ordeal should occur after the summer holidays, yet well before Christmas when the family would be around again, and as quietly as possible, she also seemed to me, in the fantasy of my imagination, to have selected for her death the moment when at last I was enjoying some security. She had watched me, with worried grey eyes, through the financially uncertain years of a writer's life and other difficulties. I am thankful that she closed those eyes, if close them she had to, at a moment when it might have seemed to her that at last she could relax her vigil.

What of her fastidiousness? What of the allied clinging to youth, with its greater wholesomeness of the flesh and its power to continue in healthy physical pursuits? Her life of hard routine work, writing, painting, music, gardening, swimming, tennis, boating, sobriety, regular hours, had enabled her well to resist the years. She used sparingly that make-up that so often, contrary to intention, only hardens the features and gives a raddled look to those no longer young. And wholesome, and swiftly, she died. No slow wasting disease presented her to her family as she would not wish to have been seen. No extreme age, though I learnt after her death that she was in her eighties, crippled her. A graceful lady, not asking to be waited on but waiting upon others, she remained to the end, and so — was gone.

One moment she had been waving me goodbye, her face sad as always on such occasions; the next, stunned, I was listening at my place of work to my elder sister Eileen's voice over the phone, with only her sobs and her question, 'Can't you guess?' (the word 'dead' was never mentioned), to make me believe the unbelievable, admit to my brain the inadmissible; and hardly afterwards, after a nightmare night passed with my heart hammering, and a journey, I was outside the hospital, witnessing the horrifying sight of the coffin appearing round the angle of the building. My mother, my darling mother, lying in that varnished box!

My father, broken, hardly able to speak, supported on either side, had insisted on seeing her in her coffin. Eileen and I refused; we wished to remember her as we had last seen her. I think that my mother would not have wished for us to see her so. And always, oh

176

always, her children must be spared any shock. I learnt that she had been convalescing well, sitting in a chair writing letters. Suddenly she was found lying across her bed gasping. Doubtless a blood clot from the operation wound had found its way into the lung. My younger sister Maureen, emerging from giving anaesthetics in the operating theatre, was told the news by a scared young nurse. Maureen hurried to the scene. She found the house surgeon doing all that could be done. She herself tried mouth-to-mouth respiration, but my mother's breathing stopped and then her heart stopped.

So it was that we found ourselves driving the hundred and fifty miles and more to Kinsale in Maureen's car. My father was seated beside her in front, and Eileen and I behind. On my lap were my mother's soft coat and some other clothes. My mother had been looking forward eagerly, in her letters, to this homecoming. Now she was travelling down before us in her hearse, through a red-brown sunshine autumn day that she, a gardener and artist, could not see.

What a miserable finish is death! A complex of physical appearances and mental attributes, that form a personality, an individual precious to some family, suddenly with a blank finality wiped off the surface of the earth like a picture sponged off a blackboard! 'A merciful release' is the hackneyed tribute paid to death in some circumstances. What a tribute! That the final condition of a person was so miserable, that the bleak pathetic little resolution of death was to be preferred! Little wonder that so many invent their religions and their fantasies of a future life, to take away from the stark and merciless denouement of the grave.

Nature's indifferent final solution, which it inflicts no less on the most intelligent of human beings, with their immense capacity to realise and therefore to suffer, than on the most ruminative of cows — nature's solution is no man's fault. The ceremony at the graveside, built up upon the tears of millions down the centuries, was sensitive and decent, shaped to the needs of grief. The professional mourners who had made the arrangements knew how to behave. Everything that human sensibility could do: in gravity, in the simple ceremony of the clergyman, in the dutiful attendance of fifty relatives and friends, in the morning-dew freshness of flowers completely covering the new-formed mound of earth, was done to disguise the fact that, as one turned to go, one was leaving behind one's mother buried like a dog in a hole.

For my sisters, doubtless, it was otherwise. So too for my poor father when I visited his room. He was reading his Bible, as was his evening custom. He lay in one of the twin beds on his side, holding up the book as a screen, a last lamp of hope, between him and that other terrible empty bed. But his distraught eyes could scarcely focus the print. In the days that followed, he endured the pain of living through his deeply-held religion and a dedication to the task of celebrating the memory of my mother.

Back at my place of work, I typed and sent to him innumerable copies of an account in which he had set forth, with a hand slowed by what he took to be arthritis but which more probably was the muscle wastage of age, the circumstances of her death. These, with a brief covering letter, he sent out far and wide. He ordered a stained-glass window to be prepared. When the work went slowly, he became at one point unreasonably peremptory. Yet one could sympathise; he could not but feel, in his late eighties, that time which was before others was not before him.

He was, alas, right. Only a few months later I was again receiving a message over that atrocious telephone, this time a dictated wire. A fearful motor-car accident it seemed to indicate. The wording was obscure. Was it as good as a notice of his death? I felt sickened by this gesture of fate, this sweep of its insensate arm with which it had brushed my parents off the face of the globe, the unfeeling foot-tread with which it had stamped out a home, my joy in sunshine and refuge in rain, without which I had never known life. A hundred times I read between the lines of the telegram, always trying to discover hope. 'Suspected fracture . . .' Would they prove to be fractures? If so, how bad were the fractures?

A letter arrived from Maureen. Some weeks back she had set out on the long sea voyage to take up a hospital appointment in India. She should be there about now. I could hardly believe my eyes when I saw the address at the head of the letter; she was in Kinsale at our father's house! She had, over weeks, made her way across the sea, then over days by train across the Indian sub-continent, only to find a cable awaiting her which caused her to have to fly back to the very point from which she had set out. Her letter advised me to come at once. That was the end of reading much hope between the lines.

I entered the front door of the hospital in Cork, my breathing short. Thither he had been brought by ambulance the twenty miles from Kinsale. What should I find? 'Is he alive?' were almost my first words to the porter in the office. 'Oh yes, he's alive.' The porter filled his voice with reassurance. I was up the stairs and pushing open the door of the private room. At the sound, my father turned his head. I had left behind an elderly gentleman always well groomed. I returned to an aged husk. His hair was tousled, his chin unshaven. Through his open mouth, bereft of its dentures, he drew in his slightly congested breath. In this burnt-up profile, outlined against the window beyond, I could hardly recognise my poor father.

The toughest and most manly of men (and yet, below, the most instantly moved when anyone was ill or in financial distress), he had never allowed me to kiss him since I had entered my teens. Now, in my horrified pity, I crossed to the high iron bed and kissed him on the cheek. He seemed to understand. When, on visiting him the following day with my sisters, I made to repeat the greeting, he drew back with a gesture and a half uttered sound of protest that left me disturbed. I rapidly turned my greeting into a pressure of my hand on his. In this fashion I approached him every morning or afternoon in the long weary days, growing into weeks, that lay before him.

On this first day, when I had rounded his bed to sit on a chair on the other side, I studied him afresh. In the warm spring light now falling on his face, no longer a silhouette, I began to recognise my father once again. Once again I could trace in his features their old aspect of strength. There were bruises on his face, but they mostly cleared up in a few days. The damage, the terrible damage, of multiple fractures and a destroyed knee joint, that was sapping his strength, lay deceptively hidden beneath the fair exterior of the bedclothes. From a bar above his head, running the length of the bed, hung a loop of material. Into this he kept his left arm hooked, so that he could shift his position from time to time.

When Maureen had sent for Eileen and myself, he seemed to have but a day or two to live. But a change of treatment instituted by Maureen, who had the advantage over the hospital doctor, whom she knew, of a prior knowledge of our father's constitution, had wrought a great improvement. It was good to see the strength with which that bare arm, the pyjama sleeve slipped down it, hauled upon the loop of cloth. But, as the days passed, the skin began to hang looser and looser on his arm like a withered drapery. He began to require help in shifting his position. The once sturdy frame beneath the pyjama jacket seemed, under my hands, daily punier. 'These fracture cases always lose a lot of weight,' said Maureen. Eileen had, at this time, returned to her job.

Yes, my father's going fitted his life. A tough give-away-nothing warrior, barking at his office servants and his gangs of coolies in his former days as an engineer in India, at his children sometimes, at those who worked for him since his retirement, domineering if allowed to be, unswerving in his beliefs, mixing with his tenderness towards grief or illness a certain unimaginativeness and insensitivity, in short, sufficiently sure that his way was the only way, to be a natural boss, his end was embattled, racked, merciless.

His sturdy constitution, built up on a lifetime of abstinence, enormously hard work, regular hours, allowed him to die only by inches. Waves of pain from his foot, as it seemed to him, but in reality referred pain from his fractures, forced him to draw in his breath. When he looked out of the window at the tops of the houses and trees of the town, he saw a world that no longer contained the wife who for more than fifty years had scarcely been from his side. It was hard enough to watch his restlessness and pain for the hour or two that we were there. It was almost impossible to let one's mind dwell on the hours he had thus spent since the last visit. Yet, brave beyond all bravery, he fought it out without weakening, ready to die, yet desiring to live to see the installation of the window in the church.

Only once did he show the fatigue of battle. A sob in his voice, he quoted some passage from the Bible, adding, 'It's a great comfort.' Once he said, 'I'm glad that Mum is dead; she couldn't have stood this.' It didn't seem to occur to him that she wouldn't have been standing at his bedside watching him, but would have been lying, probably even more fearfully injured, in another bed herself. For it is inconceivable that, as he drove back from morning church, she wouldn't have been at his side. It was a woman in a cottage that first saw the car, its engine still running, striking the stone wall of the family house Raffeen where its corner jutted out at the sharp downhill corner, bouncing back, and so striking it again. The front of the car was concertina-ed in upon my father. It can hardly be doubted that my mother, without her hands upon a steering-wheel to support her, would have been flung through the windshield. The woman who found my father sponged the blood from his face until the doctor could be fetched. An ambulance took him to Cork.

To the end, he retained the lucidity of a first-rate mind. Often he called for documents, though he was too weak to deal with them when they were brought. Only once did his mind wander for a moment. Summoning all his strength, for he was finding it ever harder to speak, he informed a visitor that he had received a letter saying that my mother's eldest brother, a retired judge in South Africa, was dead as the result of a car accident. This brother had indeed a short while back, on a visit to my mother and father, suffered a severe car accident. But, after weeks in a hospital in Cork, he had recovered and returned to South Africa.

When we pointed out to our father that he could have got no post the day before, Easter Monday, that there was no post by his bedside that morning, and that it must have been a dream, he became quite annoyed, or at least distressed. He said that he thought that he had drafted a reply. (We had to support his hand for him to sign essential documents.) To ease his mind, I made enquiries in the hospital. There had been no letter. Then he said it might have been a telegram. There was no telegram or phoned message. When I told him this, he gazed at me so long and searchingly that I had to look away. Did he now realise that he might have been dreaming of his own death? (We heard later from my mother's brother that he was in good health.) Had my father discovered in the course of his life, as I had in mine, how the sleeping mind, shying away from a contemplation too painful for it, substitutes instead some close parallel?

Indeed, it *was* the day of his death. If I had not realised, over the past three days, that he was staging his last fight, it was because of a conflict in the evidence of his symptoms, and because we lacked one essential piece of information. At the time my mind dwelt chiefly on the good symptoms, though occasionally it brooded over the others. On the first of the last three days I noticed that the loop of cloth, into which he could hook his arm to ease his position, had been put out of his way over the bar. Was he so much more comfortable that he didn't need it, or so much weaker that he couldn't use it? I dared not ask, and hoped the first.

I clasped his hand as usual where it lay, and noticed that it was cold. He could hardly open his eyes, but we thought that this drowsiness might be due to drugs. Maureen, while keeping an eye on his treatment, had, as a doctor concerned with the patient of another doctor, to move with circumspection; she herself had suffered interference on occasion when treating a patient with doctor relatives. As usual, I surreptitiously glanced at his chart. It still mentioned nothing in the way of the administration of drugs, except that of digitalis to support the heart. It was encouraging to notice that his very high pulse rate had at last come down sharply, then ominous to perceive that this had been achieved only by doubling the dose of digitalis. The next day, for the first time, the chart was not in the room. Again his hand was cold.

Yet other portends had been good. I thought that he might have turned the corner. On reaching Cork from Kinsale the following day I bought my ticket home. I made no decision to use it until I had seen him. When we entered, I noticed that his letters beside him were unopened. This had never been so before. But his face! It bore upon it such an expression of utter exhaustion, such a shine of cold sweat, as I had never seen before. The longer I gazed upon that face, weary with its twenty-five-day-long struggle, covered with a many-days' growth of beard (at his better moments they had shaved him, but towards the end they left him alone) the more impossible it became to believe that he would survive.

I moistened a sponge under the basin tap. To my enquiry as to whether he would like his face sponged, he faintly nodded his agreement. All my wiping seemed to do nothing to remove that cold glisten. He listened to his letters and the newspaper editorial. Despite his lethargy, his mental grip was complete, for the only time he spoke it was to whisper to me, 'When are you travelling?' The subject been not been mentioned since the day before.

When two nurses arrived to give him his morning clean-up, we went outside and sat on a seat in the passage way. The sister arrived to join the nurses. As she passed us, she shook her head hopelessly. Maureen asked her if he was being given any drugs to account for his drowsiness. She replied that he was being given nothing except the digitalis. From that moment I knew that he was finished. The sister and nurses had not been with him more than a minute or two, when the door opened and the sister said urgently, 'Doctor, there's been a sudden change.'

Maureen hurried in. I followed. Our father was on his back, his mouth open, gasping. Maureen took his pulse with one hand, placed the other over his heart, and now and then shifted this hand to lift his eyelid. After a while she said, 'There's nothing there.' She held up his jaw to close his mouth, and the sister held it up on the other side. Our father, with a pause between them, drew in two long sobbing breaths.

My horror must have been reflected in my face, for I became aware that one of the nurses was watching me. The loudspeaker in the passage began to call out, 'Dorman.' The nurse who had been watching me went out. The other put a roll of cotton-wool under my father's chin, so that Maureen and the sister could let it go. It occurred to me, the only layman in the room, among these others moving about with professional knowledge, that all this was being done so that his mouth might be closed when the muscles stiffened in death.

Yet I, seeing for the first time a man die, didn't know for certain whether he was dead or not, so indeterminate was the actual moment of ceasing, so piecemeal were the processes of dissolution. I remembered, when I had first entered the room that morning, noticing at once how his hands, once so broad and now so thin, once so involved in the manual labours of a handiman and now so stiff, were clutched like rigid claws about the top edge of the sheet. He was staring at them. Presently I saw him trying to straighten his bent fingers, but there was hardly any movement. The weakening heart-beat was unable to supply the extremities; his hands were all but dead upon the living body.

The nurse, who had gone out, returned to say that I was wanted on the telephone. But when she and I had got as far as the loudspeaker, it was to learn that there was someone down in the entrance hall to see me. I said to her, 'They'll ask me about my father. What am I to tell them? Is there any pulse at all?' 'Oh, I think he must be dead now.' The caller was a relative who said she came in every day to inquire after my father. I gave the news.

I returned to find Maureen in the passage. I asked her, 'Is he dead?' She replied, 'Oh yes, he's dead.' I asked her to fetch some belongings out of the room, and she did so. I thought: No, I'm not going to say goodbye to Dad like this, and I went in and kissed his poor forehead. It was still warm. Death was less terrible than I had supposed, so gradual was the fading of living into non-living. I heard my sister ask the nurse to put a clean pair of pyjamas on him over those that he was already wearing. I had always had vague ideas of winding-sheets; so it was in pyjamas that one entered the bed of the grave!

The doctor appeared, holding the missing chart. He pointed out how, every time our father's pulse-rate had been brought down by digitalis, it had returned to a point ever higher. The struggle had been too much for an eighty-six-year-old heart.

I returned to Raffeen alone. Maureen had to meet a guest who couldn't be put off. I found that the whole of Kinsale knew already; the cousin in the hospital vestibule had evidently been busy on the telephone. I couldn't sleep that night for the vision of my poor father's exhausted unshaven face, his mouth open gasping for breath. In the space of six months my father and mother swept away, and my home empty! I kept out of his study, his bedroom, his safes, his private papers, all of his holies of holies. I should have felt like a traitor going anywhere near them, with him helpless to defend them; like a Vandal rifling a temple. I wired to my elder sister Eileen.

Next day, when Marueen and I arrived at the hospital, it was to find there the rector, the people in charge of the funeral, a family friend, and the hearse. If I had the day before seen for the first time a man die, I now for the first time saw a man dead in his coffin. He lay there with lace covering his body, and parted to show his face. He looked less terrible, for they had shaved him and cleaned him up; indeed, he looked peaceful and frozen-pale.

In procession we drove down to Kinsale. I shouldered the coffin with the gravediggers, and we placed it in the Church of St. Multose at a point just before the choir stalls. Eileen had arrived. There was a brief service; the main service was to take place the next day. For the second night I hardly slept, and this time because of a vision of a wax-pale face strangely set in lace — my father, a tough give-nothing-away warrior with no frills.

Chief Engineer, Roads and Buildings, of the Pubjab in India before his retirement, a leading lay figure in his Church, a commissioner in the Boy Scout Movement, head of his branch of an old local family, he drew, with these advantages of masculine prestige, twice as many mourners to his graveside as did my mother, and the Bishop also. For the second time I watched a parent being lowered into one of those wretched little holes in the ground. My sisters and I left our parents' house one by one, the dogs were taken away, even the garage was empty for the car had been a total wreck, and silence descended upon a home.

When I returned months later, it was to find the gravelled drive with weeds and poppies growing on it two and three feet high, and almost as thick as the flowers and weeds in the beds. No gravestone, no tablet, no stained-glass window, could have spoken so heart-rendingly of dear devoted hands departed; of the speed with which the jungle closes in the instant the human race ceases its ceaseless war against it. So ends all in the ineptitude of cessation, the mismanagement of the grave, the cruel black-plumed farce of death.

END

Brigid and the Mountain
Sean Dorman

On my right was the mighty and bare peak of Mount Shanhoun, in shape and proportion an almost perfect pyramid. Brigid stood by the door watching me. She wore a plaid kerchief over her head and tied under her chin.

Agnes's buxom body might have become more buxom, as her mother Brigid alleged, yet secretly I was attracted by it. She was so compact, so rounded, so sturdy and vigorous, so shapely, yes, even graceful, as she moved rhythmically, as I had seen her one day weeding a field of potatoes.

Under its first title of 'Valley of Graneen', before a revision, *Brigid and the Mountain* was Recommended by the Book Society. *The Times Literary Supplement*, after a long review, summed up the book in the phrase, 'beautiful restraint'. *The Scotsman* wrote, 'His sketches are vivid and sincere. The physical aspects of the valley are described with remarkable clarity, and Mr Dorman is equally successful in his portraits of the inhabitants.' *The Sydney Morning Herald* wrote, in the course of a review of over two hundred words, 'These sketches of Donegal are delightful.' *Irish Independent*: 'Of his days in the valley, his friendships, and his talks, (Sean Dorman) has moulded a book of much charm. There is writing of grace and high degree . . . Withal, it is a notable book.' *Irish Press*: 'Sean Dorman brought with him a receptive mind, an artists's observant eye, and some writing materials. The result is . . . a very pleasant book.'

ISBN 0 9518119 8 3   Price £4.99

The Raffeen Press

Red Roses for Jenny
Sean Dorman

Red Roses for Jenny . . . What did they mean to her? A father's affection? Or a lover's desire? If they meant either to her, or both to her, then why did she throw them away? Did her mother come to hear of them? Or the wife of the man who gave them to her? And Jim, what did he think? He must have seen them, and surely he must have been disturbed. Was Jenny carrying a child, or was she not? If she were, could Jim succeed on containing the scandal and so protect his mother's feelings? Canon Moss, for all his funny ways, was wise. Was his wisdom sufficient to save them all? And, at the end of the long day, why did Jenny restore the red roses to her office desk again?

After the great success of Sean Dorman's autobiographical first novel, *Brigid and the Mountain*, initially, until revised, entitled 'Valley of Graneen' and, under that title, a Book Society Recommendation; also praised by *The Times Literary Supplement*, *The Irish Press*, *The Scotsman*, Australia's *Sydney Morning Herald*, *Irish Independent*, and many others; Mr Dorman took time off to acquire the technique of the non-autobiographical novel. The result is *Red Roses for Jenny*, with its vivid characters and driving speed of narrative. If the mountain scapes of *Brigid and the Mountain* are fine, no less fine are the seascapes of *Red Roses for Jenny*, with storm scenes as background to a love between a man and a woman no less stormy.

ISBN 0 9518119 7 5   Price £4.99

The Raffeen Press

Portrait of My Youth
Sean Dorman

Portrait of My Youth traces the earlier years of a remarkable Irish writer, Sean Dorman. The narrative, always lively, often extremely funny, sweeps the reader along on a bubbling current. There are fascinating glimpses of the British Raj in India as seen through a young child's eyes; of Algiers and Aden as seen through those of an older schoolboy; of student escapades at Oxford and in Paris in a more carefree era; of a visit to an extraordinary French family near Nice and Cannes: of sexual shenanigans in London's bohemian Chelsea; of difficulties with an alcoholic uncle famous as an Irish playwright; of meetings with literary and theatrical notables: E. M. Forster, Granville Barker, Sean O'Casey, John Betjeman, T. S. Eliot, Barry Fitzgerald, Dame Sybil Thorndike, W. B. Yeats, Laurence Olivier, Deborah Kerr.

'Delightful, humorous, full of marvellous observation.'
Colin Wilson

At the age of fourteen, in his first term at his public school, Sean Dorman was awarded a prize as the best prose writer in the school. He was the winner of an essay competition open to the public schools of Great Britain and Ireland. After graduating at Oxford, he worked as a freelance journalist in London, contributing articles to some twenty periodicals, and ghosting six non-fiction books for a publisher. For five and a half years he edited a theatrical and art magazine in Dublin, and for twenty-six years in England a magazine for writers. His three-volume hardback, *The Selected Works of Sean Dorman*, comprises autobiography, essays, novels, short stories and verse.

ISBN 0 9518119 9 1   1 Price £4.99

The Raffeen Press

The Madonna
Sean Dorman

'English life through Irish wit.'

Judy Summers, arrested by the sound of men's voices, paused on her way to visit The Madonna. Her cheap gay cotton dress fluttered about her shapely legs. Judy Summers liked men. She liked them very much. Also, it had become imperative that she should acquire a husband . . .

They were beside the little wayside shrine. George saw that Judy's eyes were fixed on the painted Mother cradling in her arms her painted Baby. 'The birth and the feeding have been a great strain on you, darling. Don't you think that Mark ought to go on to the bottle?' Judy was shaking her head vigorously. 'I'd give my life for Mark. I feel — I feel there's something in me of The Madonna.'

George went to Rose. She drew away in hurt pride. He broke down her resistance and swept her into his arms. 'Of course you didn't mean any harm, sweetheart. I've had a very upsetting letter from Judy. I love my wife. She's the mother of my son, but it's been a great strain. You've helped me keep my sanity.' He began to rain down kisses on her brow, her cheeks, her lips. Eyes closed, she held up her face to receive them.

'*The Madonna* reads as inevitably as does Tolstoy and bears out Eliot's, "In my end is my beginning." If it reaches its proper audience, it will be read with a mixture of discovery and relief. The novel is still alive!'
George Sully

ISBN 0 9518119 6 7   Price £4.99

The Raffeen Press

Physicians, Priests & Physicists
Sean Dorman

The most potent reason for Sean Dorman's writing this book arose from the existence of his magazine *Commentary*. This monthly appeared in Dublin in the forties during five and a half years. At an average of two thousand copies a month, he felt it to be a certainly that copies still lurked in collections both public and private, even possibly in newspapers files, there to haunt him. In his youthful, pugnacity, had he somtimes overstated his ease and fallen into folly? If so, the only way out was to republish his essays or editorials, with inserted toning down remarks where such seemed needed.

The essays cover the subjects of: literary censorship; cancer, heart disease and arthritis-resisting diets and exercises, including exercises underwater in a hot bath (his wife suffered from arthritis of the hip, and died of smoking and alcohol-induced cancer); the existence or non-existence of God as found in the Bible; or in the discoveries about the universe as found in the work of scientists such as Aristotle, Ptolemy, Copernicus, Galileo, Kepler, Newton, Einstein (his Special Theory, and his General Theory, of Relativity, are explained in simple terms), and the somewhat later quantum mechanics, and the twistor and superstring theories. Other essays are entitled: 'How to Rear a Baby', 'The Adventures of Marriage', 'Jew and Gentiles'.

ISBN 0 9518119 1 6   Price £5.95

The Raffeen Press

The Strong Man
Sean Dorman

The Strong Man, a comedy in three acts, can lay no claims either to distinction or to having been performed on a stage. But it can claim to have been read by a considerable number of people who have reported that it caused them not only to smile but, on occasion, to laugh outright. Should something that has given rise to smiles, and even laughter, be left upon a shelf, or be entombed in a drawer? Of course not. It should be produced in a book. Also produced in this book are three theatre critiques. In days gone by, Ireland gave to literature great playwrights from that seeming hotbed of dramatic genius, Dublin University: William Congreve, George Farquhar, Oliver Goldsmith. Since then there have been: John Millington Synge, Samuel Beckett (both from the same university), William Butler Yeats, Oscar Wilde, Bernard Shaw, Sean O'Casey. Well known, but perhaps less well known than they ought to be, are Denis Johnston and Teresa Deevy. I have devoted a critique to each of them. Also to William Shakespeare, an Englishman, I'm told. The trouble with William Shakespeare, is that he has been allowed, unfortunately, to develop into a cult figure. Not only are his great plays produced, but his lesser pieces also are reverently laid out upon the stage, thus almost certainly denying many hours of theatre time to others with better work to offer. Such a lesser piece, here reviewed, is *Twelve Night*.

ISBN 0 9503455 6 3   Price £3.95

The Raffeen Press